STORIES BY FANS FOR FANS

DAVE
MATTHEWS
BAND

STORIES BY FANS FOR FANS

DavE MatthewS BanD

EDITED BY ARIEL CHERNIN

The publication of *Dave Matthews Band FanFare*
has been generously supported by
the Government of Canada through the
Book Publishing Industry Development Program.

CANADIAN CATALOGUING IN PUBLICATION DATA

ISBN 1-55022-417-4
1. Dave Matthews Band. I. Chernin, Ariel.
ML421.D246D24 2000   782.42166'092'2   C00-931715-5

Front cover photo by Sydney Burtner / *The Observer*
Back cover photo by Mary Spiro.
Cover and interior design by Guylaine Régimbald.
This book is set in Trade Gothic and Compress Sans.

Printed by Transcontinental Printing, Peterborough, Ontario, Canada.

Second printing.

Distributed in Canada by General Distribution Services,
325 Humber College Blvd., Etobicoke, Ontario M9W 7C3.

Distributed in the United States by LPC Group,
1436 West Randolph Street, Chicago, Illinois, 60607. U.S.A.

Distributed in Europe by Turnaround Publisher Services, Unit 3,
Olympia Trading Estate, Coburg Road, Wood Green, London N2Z 6T2

Distributed in Australia and New Zealand by Wakefield Press
17 Rundle Street (Box 2266), Kent Town, South Australia 5071

Published by ECW PRESS,
2120 Queen Street East, Suite 200,
Toronto, Ontario M4E 1E2.

ecwpress.com

PRINTED AND BOUND IN CANADA

Contents

Joshua Hancock	62
Alex Effgen	63
Stacey Borelli	66
Jen Nagel	67
Jeff Lewis	67
Mike Hayes	68
Sophie Boddington	69
Maria Gaston	70
Ann Sentz	70
Pete Asher	71
Susan Davis	72
Alisa Hoyt	72
Erin Tietje	74
Cindy Cline	75
Richard Gericke	76
Jamie Morrison	76
Brian Wohlert	77
Dana Robustelli	77
Jamie Santistevan	79
Patrick Acton	80
Jonathan Guez	81
Jeff Smith	82
Todd Pace	82
Kyle Smith	84
Brooke Lotz	86
Sean Smith	87
Josh Hughes	88
Matt Iorlano	89
Matt Anderson	90
Ryan Krause	91
Charcee Starks	93
Yehuda Goldman	94
Cristie Capaldi	94
Paul Lemire	95
Brian Phillips	96
Erin Pallone	97
John Grant	99

ACKNOWLEDGMENTS

First and foremost, I'd like to thank the fans who contributed to this book. Their stories and photos *are DMB FanFare*, and their enthusiasm and kindness made putting this book together an amazing experience. The Dave Matthews Band is lucky to have such devoted fans.

Thank you to Stof for his tireless efforts on the Internet and to Mika Goodfriend and Nat Hebert for their work on the *DMB FanFare* website. Thanks also to John Sakell and Adnan Ghanchi for their technical assistance. I'm also grateful to Mary Williams for her editorial insight and to Guylaine Régimbald for her innovative design ideas.

A special thanks to everyone at ECW Press for their guidance and support. In particular, I'd like to thank Robert Lecker for giving me the opportunity to work on this project and Holly Potter for imparting her knowledge of the publishing industry.

—Ariel Chernin

FOREWORD

I've been a fan of the Dave Matthews Band since August 12, 1995, the day that DMB performed at the County Bowl in Santa Barbara, California. Knowing absolutely nothing about the band, I had bought tickets to the show on a whim, after reading an interview with Dave in a local paper. To put it mildly, the concert blew me away. I had never heard anything as musically intense as DMB and spent 2 1/2 hours dancing like a maniac. It was — and remains — one of the best live performances I've ever seen. I've since become a loyal DMB fan: I have all the CDs, I'm somewhat well-versed in DMB history, and I've been lucky enough to attend another live show (Montreal 05/02/98). But in spite of all this, my love for the band pales in comparison to the passion and enthusiasm expressed in this book. *DMB FanFare* puts me to shame.

Beginning with Nat Felder's lyrical ode to the DMB fan and ending with Kari Johnson's humorous encounter with Stefan Lessard, *FanFare*'s 105 contributing writers proclaim a fierce devotion to all things DMB. To get the band to play "#40," Ryan Krause printed up 300 signs and passed them out to fans in Chicago's United Center. Timothy Harden instigated a high-speed chase with the DMB tour bus just so he could say Hi to Dave. Missy Davidson ate Dave's leftover broccoli! Many fans, like Carolyn Sabbatelli and Andrew Rachmiel, simply wanted to thank the band for their music and its positive impact.

I was happy to learn that the fans' intense gratitude and support is definitely appreciated by the members of DMB. Dave, Boyd, Carter, Stefan, and Leroi treat their fans like close friends. Danielle Havasi has chatted on-line with Boyd, and Carter once asked Brittany Tobar for her autograph!

In total, we received an astounding 575 *DMB FanFare* submissions and I enjoyed reading each and every one. (Okay, I probably could have done without the accounts of sexual acts performed to the music of DMB, but they did make for interesting reading.) While it would be impossible to publish all 575 stories, *DMB FanFare* exists because of **everyone** who participated.

COME DANCE WITH ME

Just about anyone can relate to my story. The music of the Dave Matthews Band pulls you in, and you make a connection to it. You can feel the solid rhythm of Stefan and Carter, the percussive strumming of Dave, the melodic sax work of Leroi, and the explosive outbursts of Boyd's violin. It is for these reasons that I am a DMB fan. I get strange stares on my trips to school and back each day. Before each journey to and from school, I whip out my faithful, scratched, dented, and barely alive Walkman, and I pop in the daily live tape of DMB. I don't drive to school, and I don't walk either. I take more of a Dave Matthews Band approach.

As I go out the front door, the heavenly music starts to take effect. It all starts with a little head bob to the beat. The hands soon start moving to the tempo. There is no turning back; it has taken control. It continues to move downward. Soon, from the waist up, everything is bobbing and bouncing to the beat. I can't hold back any longer; my feet start to twitch. My knees go up and down, my heels bounce outward, and I rotate upon my toes in Dave Matthews fashion. I bounce, jump, and spin my way to school. As Carter beats away on the intro to "#36," I join in on my air-drum set with an abnormally large smile. As Stefan works his groove on "The Song That Jane Likes," I'm there with him, bouncing my head and squeezing my eyes shut as he hits a slide. As Leroi makes his sax sing in "Lie in Our Graves," my fingers fly up and down my imaginary sax. As Dave sings away in "#41," my head swings from side to side and I squish my face into the most painful expressions along with him. And, finally, as Boyd erupts in "Tripping Billies" or "Dancing Nancies," I erupt as well, jumping up and down and madly fiddling on a violin that doesn't exist.

As I make my way through the downtown district, babies cry, small animals run and hide, mothers shield their children's eyes, and everyone — from fourteen year olds with neon-green hair to the eighty-year-old man reading the paper and finishing off his fifth pack of the day — gives me the most confused, uneasy, astonished, uncomfortable, perplexed, shocked, restless, puzzled look in existence. These reactions, however, I ignore. They cannot hear, nor understand, the musical utopia that I am experiencing. I just keep on dancing and doing my thing. My name is Nat Felder, and I don't care how many looks I get. I am a Dave Matthews Band fan.

— *Nathaniel Felder*

BEST OF WHAT'S AROUND

Anybody who's ever been to a Dave Matthews Band show knows that you can walk into a venue in the worst of moods, and right when the guys step onstage—and Dave says "Hi, y'all" and hits the first couple of chords on his guitar—you forget about that fight you had with your boyfriend or the fact that you're broke and you just bought second-row tickets with the money you should have used to fix your car. We've all grown to know and love the band's songs as if we wrote them ourselves. We sing every word, and we know when Boyd is going to start playing that violin like it's the last time he'll ever play it again. And although we know it's coming, somehow Carter still knocks us on our asses with his amazing drum-playing capabilities. And in the shadows, Stefan and Leroi hold it all together without breaking a sweat.

My love for the band is ever growing. I've known of them and loved them since late '94. My first DMB show was in May of '95, when the guys opened up for the Grateful Dead. I was only fifteen then, but somehow I knew that these guys were going to be *big!* I walked out of the Silver Bowl in Las Vegas, Nevada, with a newfound respect for music and for the five guys from C'ville. I wouldn't see the band live again until the summer of '96, when they hooked up with the H.O.R.D.E. festival.

I remember standing with my friends in one-hundred-and-fifteen-degree heat, surrounded by drunken people who were pushing and shoving the crowd in every direction. When the band came on, Dave said hi, picked up his guitar, and started playing "#41." Anybody who knows me knows about my love for that song. And everyone around me could have seen (if they were looking hard enough), pure excitement coming from my inside out. I was one happy girl! Unfortunately, I was pushed out of the crowd, escaping with cuts and bruises given to me by some demented lady with fingernails of steel. I was so upset that I started crying from frustration.

We left early and headed back to our hotel. Once we got there we headed towards the pool, and we saw a dark-purple bus pulling up. The most impossible thing to me at that time was meeting the band, and in an instant it all became possible. The guys were staying in the rooms right across from ours. The only thing that divided us was a parking lot. I was so ecstatic! Dave got off, said hi, and went into his room. Then off came Carter, Boyd, Stefan, and some roadies. I ran up to Carter, and somewhere between shaking and saying, "Oh my God, you're so amazing," I asked him for his autograph. He agreed and began writing these words: "Nora, keep on jammin'. We love you! Carter Beauford." Then Stefan came over and signed my binder. Dave eventually came out of his room, and we all took pictures and talked for more than an hour. We let them go on their way. But Carter stayed behind and talked to us for almost two hours about the band and about music. He is so friendly. When you're talking to him you feel like he really wants to be there in that exact moment talking to you. Carter is what I remember most about that night. To make a very long story short, Carter eventually joined the rest of the band at the pool. The next morning we thanked them for everything, and they were off to the next show. Every time I see DMB live it still feels the same. I never get tired of seeing them or hearing them. Their music means so much to so many people. And if they are reading this, we thank you for your music. Even if you don't realize it, you do so much for all of us. You're the "best of what's around!"

— *Nora Fitzsimmons*

THE ULTIMATE
SUMMER JOB
During the summer of 1997, I worked for the Dave Matthews Band. Seriously — I did. It was at Lakewood Amphitheater in Atlanta, Georgia, and I was what you might call a gofer — in actuality, a production assistant. When the band was on a tour stop in Atlanta, I literally ran into Dave Matthews. I was excited about working for them that day, and at about ten in the morning I was turning the corner in the dressing-room hall, and I ran into this thing. I looked up to see Dave Matthews. I uttered an apology, and he said it helped him wake up. So we went on with our day. I couldn't stop staring at the band. Carter was flamboyant; Stefan and Leroi were quiet and reclusive.

Boyd needed to work out at a gym. My boss asked me to drive him to a local gym in the rich area of Atlanta. So I did — did I want to get fired for not doing my job? Anyway, we got stuck in traffic and I asked him a bunch of questions relating to the history of the band and where Peter Greisar was these days. I dropped him off, and the best was yet to come. Around four that afternoon, I was hanging out with their sound man as he was getting ready for the sound check. Well, the band walked out and my jaw dropped. I was about to watch a Dave Matthews Band sound check! They started off with "Rhyme & Reason," and I started off dancing. I wasn't working any-more—I was playing. After "R & R," they started playing this new song, but I didn't know what it was. It started off with a baseline that was funky, but it sounded like a serious love song or something. Then it was over. Sound check was done and I was still grooving. Then I finally met Dave.

He walked over and said, "Hi, I'm Dave. You work here?" I replied, "Yeah, but I couldn't help myself listening to you guys. I'm Matt." "Well, Matt, what did you think about that new one?" "Dude, that baseline was great—had a real groove to it." "Thanks. Follow me." We walked down the hall where we met earlier and into his dressing room. Unfortunately, I didn't get to stay long, as I was dragged away by my boss to do a job. I never got to see or talk to Dave again, but I'll never forget that day. I've met other famous bands, like Pearl Jam and Fleetwood Mac, but that was one of the best days I had working there at Lakewood Amphitheater. And— oh, yeah—that song I heard, I recognized it later when I was at the Tabernacle for the filming of *Live at Ten Spot*. It was "Crush."

—*Matthew Cohen*

DMB FanFare Tip #1:
BECOME FRIENDS WITH CARTER

July 9, 1999 was the third time that I got to meet one of the greatest people in the world: Mr. Carter Beauford. My friends and I went to the Irvine Meadows Amphitheater that night telling ourselves that we would meet the band. Well, as we were trying to figure out how to find the backstage area, we stumbled across a gate, and who was behind it? The whole band! Yessssssss! As we were sticking our heads through the openings in the fence, more and more people start to come. Knowing that I had to make my move soon, I waved down Carter and flashed a picture of him and me from Halloween. Carter pointed and started laughing. He motioned that he'd be right over. Amazing! Relief! I knew everything would be okay because Carter means what he says.

After he was done with an interview he came over and told the people to open the gate so he could give us all hugs before he went onstage. It was so amazing! He remembered us and seemed so happy. I love that guy! He asked me if he could have the picture of him and me, and then he asked me to sign it. Can you believe it? When I think about it I still can't help smiling. Well, he asked us if we'd be at the show the next day in San

BRITTANY TOBAR

Carter, 1998

Francisco. Of course we would! So he told us that he'd put us on the list for passes and that he looked forward to seeing us. He wrote all of our names down on the back of a gift box that he had received and then left to play those drums.

After the show we drove all night. We arrived in San Francisco at eight o'clock in the morning and spent the whole day talking about how we were going to go backstage that night. Well, when we got to Shoreline, the passes weren't there. Tears! After we whined for about an hour, they finally found our passes. We all breathed again! We walked into the amphitheater like we were freaking gods. But it was sad. We weren't — so many people had passes! Oh, well — who cares. We were going to kick it with our band that night.

After the show we went backstage; it was outside and very nice. There were all these little white lights in the trees and stuff — it could not have been better. After waiting for about forty-five minutes we thought that maybe the band wasn't coming backstage that night. We were very sad and tired. But wait! All of a sudden, big Mel the security guard walked in. What? He was holding the gift box that Carter had written our six names on. "Is Brittany here?" As he called off each one of our names we all looked at each other. What was going on? "Follow me, girls." Okay! We followed

Mel on this journey through the parking lot, and then he stopped in front of that big gray tour bus! Every one of us exchanges glances; we were sure this wasn't real. Mel opened the door and said, "Hop on!" Carter was waiting there on the bus eating pizza. "Want some?" So there we were eating Carter's pizza and watching this Chris Rock special and joking with Carter about the bus's mirrored ceiling. Oh, my! Can this get better? Then ... hop... here comes Leroi ... then Boyd, then Dave! *Wow!* We were all in shock. We could not believe this was happening. How did these little California girls end up on DMB's tour bus chilling with them? *Wow!* I asked Boyd to sign some stuff for me— he is *sooooooo* nice! I was so excited. I didn't ask for a picture because I was too stiff. Here I am in front of Boyd Tinsley. He had on really cool pants, too. They were red. Then I got to talk with Leroi. He is so nice. I took my picture with the guy. Next, Dave. Yay! I got to give the guy a great big hug and take a picture with him, too. After about an hour and a half this adventure came to an end. We said our goodbyes and left. *Wow!* I love them! I love them all! I still have to meet Stefan one of these days. That was my last DMB encounter and by far the best. Thank you, Carter!

—*Brittany Tobar*

BOYD'S ON-LINE CHAT PARTNER The Dave Matthews Band has

always held a special place in my heart. In 1996 I created my first scrap-book (now there are seven) dedicated to their music. I expressed this to Dave in a letter. On February 26th, I played back the messages on my answering machine and my heart skipped a beat. Dave Matthews had left a message thanking me for all my letters. Two days later we spoke briefly about the Grammies, my age, his music, and my scrapbooks. He sent me an autographed photograph with original artwork that I'll always cherish. In November of '97, an instant message appeared on my computer screen. The sender claimed to be Boyd Tinsley. It was 4:30 in the morning and his insistence only heightened my suspicions. Still believing this was only someone pretending to be Boyd, I insisted he call me. Twenty minutes passed and I sent him an e-mail expressing that "he didn't have enough class to be Boyd." I pressed send, and at that moment the phone rang and Boyd's voice resonated over the line. It was four days before my birthday, and he sent me the most memorable birthday present: an autographed picture saying "Happy Birthday. Peace, Boyd Tinsley."

On August 8, 1998, in Indiana, I met Dave and Boyd for the first time. Suddenly, larger than life, there was Boyd. It was breathtaking to see him in person. He is so ripped, and I told him his body looked like it was molded — I couldn't resist. Then Dave appeared. We talked, and he looked at my inhaler (not a traditional kind). Looking perplexed he said, "How do you use that thing?" I tried to be comical, saying, "You twist and suck it up." He laughed and said, "I know a couple of other things you twist and suck up." When I snapped a picture of Dave's odd shoes the look on his face was a true Kodak moment.

Thanks to Dave, my dream extended to August 9th, when I was graced with their presence once again. In Toronto on November 17, 1998, I was

backstage talking to fans about my scrapbooks and waiting for the band. It seemed like forever, and in anticipation I commented, "What could be taking them so long?" Suddenly I felt a hand on my shoulder. When I turned around it

PATRICIA M. HAVASI

Danielle and Boyd, 1999

was Dave. I gasped and said, "You scared me!" Calmly he said, "I did? Why?" He was playful that evening. On December 10, 1998 I attended an edge session — a small acoustic show with Dave at a local radio station. Twenty people attended this performance; it was so exciting to see Dave in an intimate setting. As his eyes met mine, he waved. I was in awe that he'd acknowledged me. Later I attended a show where I seriously injured my ankle. Dave was in the corner when they strolled me to first aid. I tugged on his shoulder as we quickly passed by. On May 12, 1999 in Cleveland I asked Dave and Boyd to sign my cast from that accident in December, although Boyd insisted on signing my shoe. On November 20, 1998, as well as June 14, 19, and 22, 1999, Boyd came back and talked with me.

I showed Boyd a scrapbook that was partially finished in which I'd put things sent to me by fans — letters, photographs, and other creative things they wished to give the band. Also included were personal messages that I compiled at each show. The band received the book on June 22nd.

In Indiana on June 23, 1999 my friend Bob and I took a roadie out to lunch. As we were about to leave the hotel the elevator door opened and there stood Stefan and Leroi. I froze — I couldn't speak or walk. "Finally, after twenty-seven shows," I squeaked. After that meeting, something caught my peripheral vision. I turned my head as Dave appeared, walking towards us. I was absolutely speechless. We expressed how much we loved "#40," to which he replied, "I'm still trying to remember that damn song." Peace, love, good times, and jammin' 2 DMB 4 eternity.

—*Danielle Havasi*

THE BEST
BIRTHDAY EVER
On April 29, 1996 DMB announced that they would be hosting an exclusive party at Trax in Charlottesville, Virginia, on the evening when, at midnight, their third full-length album would be released. It would also be my nineteenth birthday at midnight on the same evening. Despite being in the middle of finals week of my second semester at Penn State, I was determined to celebrate those two events with DMB and their closest friends and fans. What better way to begin my twentieth year on this earth than with Carter, Dave, Leroi, Stefan, Boyd, and three hundred guests? Thanks to the help of several good friends and, of course, fellow old-school Nancies (Bobo, Chris, Pace — y'all rock!), I was able to land a ticket to the event. We had all spent the past couple of New Year's Eves with the band and been to many of their shows; now we were ready to celebrate the release of what we knew would be their record-breaking album.

Two skipped finals and a solo five-hour commute later, I arrived at one of the meccas of DMB patronage: Trax. It was exactly as I had imagined it but even better, because now the legendary venue was a reality for me. I ended up front row for the show, which was kicked off with unbelievable performances by both the acclaimed Boyd Tinsley Band and Everything—

complete with the rumbling and shaking of a train rolling by. And then it was time. It's been a few years now, so the details are a little sketchy. I don't remember the exact set list, except that the majority of the songs were from *Crash*. I do remember the nonpushing pleasantness of the crowd, and, most importantly, I remember midnight.

At midnight, *Crash* was officially released, and I was officially nineteen years old. My friend yelled up to Dave that it was my birthday, and Dave asked me what my name was. Before I knew it, he was singing a little tribute to my birthday, and he dedicated the next song to me. Best birthday ever, right? But it gets better. We waited around at Trax after the show, bumped into Boyd for a brief time, and decided that we had experienced the closest thing to bliss as we could as mortals. Then Dave emerged from the doors of the bar and headed right towards us. I thanked him for the most unbelievable birthday ever and gave him a shout-out from the Nancies. We shot the breeze for several minutes, and then Dave graciously invited my friend Ginny and me to join them back at Miller's. After cursing my age situation and the fact that I had a five-hour drive back to Happy Valley early the next morning, I regretfully declined the invitation. Being the cool, down-to-earth, generous person that he is, Dave asked if we'd be going to the Richmond performance the following evening, took our names, and told us to pick up our passes and join him and the band backstage the next night.

I've always considered myself to be a whimsical, live-in-the-moment type of gal, but, unfortunately, I was also given the attributes of being practical and logical. Going to the Richmond show the following evening would require me to skip two more finals, which forced me to seriously question my priorities. What was disputably my better judgment kicked in, and I decided to give the backstage pass to a longtime friend at UVA who was planning on going to the Richmond show. It was almost as if I had been so fortunate up to that point that I needed to share the wealth. And though I question my decision and my passing up what could've been an even more incredible experience with the entire band (I *so* wanted to meet Carter and let him know he's a modern-day Buddy Rich), I know I have absolutely no right to complain. It was the best birthday I've ever had and, I'll even venture to say, I will ever have again. So I guess I won't be able to conceal this from the parental units anymore. They've always wondered how I hacked my final exams so badly that semester.

—*Megan Smith*

STORIES THAT WOULD MAKE any DMB Fan Jealous

My friend and I are huge DMB fans. We've been to over thirty of their shows and have met the band on a few occasions. I will share with you two of our most memorable stories. The first took place in Raleigh, North Carolina. We had traveled there from Massachusetts with zero tickets to either of the shows at the Walnut Creek Amphitheater and no place to stay. We ended up getting information from a cab driver on

KATIE ZORN

Stefan and Alison, 1998

where the band was staying. As soon as we walked into the hotel lobby, there was Dave standing at the front desk. We were psyched! Many things happened that weekend involving the band, but to summarize without rambling on, this was the final outcome: we got invited to a birthday party

for Mike McDonald (the tour manager) by Coran Capshaw (the band's manager), and we partied all night with Dave and the crew. Coran also provided free tickets to one of the shows for us and four other fans we had met at the hotel. Leroi bought us drinks, and we chatted with him for an hour or so in a private booth at the club in the hotel. It was an excellent weekend.

The second story took place in Hartford, Connecticut. We were there to see a couple of Dave and Tim shows nearby, and again we had no tickets. We went to the first show hoping to find someone selling spare tickets, but we had no luck—the show was completely sold out. So we focused on obtaining tickets for the next night's show at U Conn. We came up with a plan on the way back to our hotel (which Dave and Tim were also staying at): we'd go and have a couple of drinks, and then come back to the hotel around the time when Dave's bus would be arriving from the concert. I would ask Dave how the show had been, explain that we had no tickets, and ask if he would be so kind as to give us tickets for the next night. I was a little nervous, but the worst thing he could say was no, right? When we got back from having a few drinks, we decided to wait around in the hotel bar for the bus. Just as I was turning the corner I heard a distinct voice coming from the bar: it was Dave, and he was on his way out of the bar, heading for the bathroom. The bus had gotten back a lot earlier than we had expected, and Dave was already throwing back a few in the bar. I was so caught off guard that I just said, "Hey, Dave. What are you doing?" He replied, "Going to pee, and you?" "Not much," I said — like a complete idiot! Then he walked away and said, "Cheers, Alison," like he always says. (I had met him a few times prior to this, and I have this obsessive-compulsive behavior about forcing him to remember my name. When talking to him I'm always, like, "Do you remember my name? It's Alison. Don't forget." I know it's annoying, but, hey, it worked. Now every time I see him he says, "Hello, Ms. Alison," or, "Cheers, Alison." He knows that it makes my day that he remembers me.) Anyway, I was so impressed that he still remembered my name that I forgot to ask for the tickets, but we still had until he left for the show the next day. We figured that we might not bump into him again, so we decided to write him a letter explaining that we were desperate for tickets and the show was sold out and we were wondering if there was anything he could do for us. We also included our room number, and we slipped the note under his door, which was two doors down from ours! We waited in our room patiently, and about ten minutes later the phone rang. I answered, and a voice said, "Alison?" It was Dave, and he said he'd hook us up with two tickets to the show. We were so psyched! The tickets were tenth row, and we were seated right behind Dave's mother. It was the best show I've been to, and we got the tickets from Dave himself! What a night!

Okay, sorry, but I just thought of another quick story that you might find interesting. This one took place in Montreal, Canada, on May 2, 1998. My friend Katie and I went up there for the weekend to see the Dave Matthews Band for my birthday. It was a great concert, and when it was over we happened to see the buses parked by a side door with a couple of security guards standing by. Although the security guards informed us that the band would not be coming out of those doors, we decided to wait and see for ourselves. Sure enough, about an hour later the band came out, one by one. Dave came out last. Right before he came out, I begged one of the security guards to leave at least enough space for me to stick my hand out and shake Dave's hand. The security guards were awesome, because when Dave came out they moved over and gave me a huge amount of space. I stuck my hand out, hoping he would just touch it. He touched all right, and he gave me a kiss on the lips. I was so shocked! I didn't even get to say a word to him. And that was the first of my many times meeting Dave. One last thing. Anyone can meet Dave if they try hard enough. He is the kindest person I've ever met. He loves his fans just as much as they love him. He truly appreciates everything he has and every fan he meets.

—*Alison Brown*

AN OLD SCHOOL FAN MEETS DAVE
I'm sure most of us who went to college in Virginia back in the early-to-mid nineties have similar stories about making the trek to Charlottesville or wherever this band everyone called "Dave" was playing. We may not have known a lot about the band itself, but we all knew one thing: we loved what we heard. The best part about it was (and still is) that it really gave us a claim to some music of our own. The schools in New York had their bands, there were tons in DC, North Carolina had Hootie (I still laugh at all those fights with my friends who went to school in North Caroline about who had the better band), and — for a short time — we had Dave. For that period, the Dave Matthews Band was the soundtrack to our lives.

I graduated from James Madison University in '95 and headed out to Los Angeles for a job at NBC. I started as a network page (you know, those blue-blazer-clad young men and women who manage *The Tonight Show* audience and give tours of the studio). Well, the pay was lousy, but the job certainly wasn't without its perks. Usually when a band was scheduled to appear on *The Tonight Show*, they would come and rehearse in the studio before the taping. Pages who weren't working were allowed to go in and hang out. I found out that DMB was going to appear on the show! Unfortunately, I was scheduled to be on tour duty during the rehearsal.

What was I gonna do? Now, if you watch *The Tonight Show* closely, you'll see there's always a page stationed immediately to the left of the band (to keep the fanatics away — hah!). All my coworkers knew I was a huge fan of the band. Luckily, the page supervisor thought my stalker potential was low (it was a big no-no to harass the talent), and I was able to sweet talk her into stationing me in the studio for the taping (thanks, Karyn!). Yes! Anyway, I'll never forget it. The band played "Ants Marching" with me standing just a few feet away. It really was just like being onstage with them. When the show ended I (nervously) talked to Dave and told him I was from JMU; he laughed and said he didn't know there were a lot of West Coast fans of the band (so modest).

During the performance he had broken a string. He brought that up during our conversation. Like an idiot I said, "I know! That was so cool!" He rolled his eyes (note to self: Dave's not a fan of breaking strings), and we chatted for another minute or so. A friend of mine was even able to snap a quick picture (granted, it was of the back of my head, but you can see Dave just fine). The whole experience was really great as there were tons of studio people there who wanted to talk to Dave, but he took the time to chat with a fan. Definitely one of my favorite DMB memories!

— Willie Goldman

TANYA SMITHERS AND DAVE REUNITED
(Well, Sort of)

I had won, and I was going to meet Dave. The contest rules: I was allowed to bring one friend, one thing to get auto-graphed, and no cameras. In a state of disbelief, I called my dear friend, who is part of what I jokingly call my "Dave posse." Between the two

Tamara's friend Bradley, Dave, and Tamara, 1998

of us we must have seen DMB at least seventy times. I told him of our good fortune—that we were going to meet Dave. The day came, May 29, 1998, and we contemplated what we would say, how we would act, what thanks we would give. Before I knew it the moment had arrived. Dave entered the gazebo where we were eagerly waiting, and he went from table to table, chatting with all who had struck gold. He came over to me, stuck his hand out, and, without hesitation, I introduced myself as "Tanya Smithers"—a woman from South Africa who Dave had known from his childhood (listen to the booger story he tells on tour). Dave's faced paled, and in disbelief he looked around to find support and confirmation that I was not her. I exclaimed that it was very nice to see him again, and he looked stunned: he was actually starting to believe me. After several minutes of seeing Dave completely blown away by the thought that his childhood crush was there in front of him, I smiled and told him I was kidding. The next thing I knew, we were hugging. (He thought it was great that I played a joke on him.) Dave signed my poster, and while he was doing so I thanked him. He turned to me and, *very* unexpectedly, kissed me and thanked me as well. My friend and Dave talked of shows and such, and then Dave moved on. Of course, this was not enough Dave attention for me, so I went back over to him and asked for a photo (they told us no pictures, but I had stuck a camera down my pants). He saw me reach down to get my camera, and he gently squeezed my leg, said "Of course," and posed for the snapshot. All of the miles we had traveled to enjoy DMB were captured in our beaming smiles in that picture. For this memory, I thank my friends with whom I share DMB, I thank Dave, and I especially thank Tanya Smithers.

— *Tamara Marks*

A CHANCE ENCOUNTER AT MILLER'S
My friend Joey and I were in Charlottesville, Virginia,on Friday, October 15, 1999, and we decided that we were going to check out Trax, one of the traditional Dave Matthews landmarks of the town. We got there only to find that this death-metal punk-type band was playing. Since this was not our crowd we decided to walk on over to Miller's, which was about a half-mile away. At about nine o'clock Joey went into the bar to get some beer for us and make use of the facilities while I sat at one of the tables outside in a little area they had set up since the weather was beautiful. Well, no more than a minute had passed when, coming through the downtown pedestrian mall, I saw Dave, walking all by himself.

At first I was thinking that it couldn't be him — and what luck if it was. Then, as he got closer to me, looking from side to side as he walked, I did a triple take and very calmly said, "Dave? Dave Matthews?" He turned and said, "Hey. How are you doing?" and proceeded to shake my hand. I answered, "I am doing okay," after trying to compose myself for a second. Then Dave asked me my name, and I told him my first and last name without even realizing it. He then repeated my name to make sure he'd got it, but he repeated it very much like he knew it from somewhere before. Obviously we'd never met before, but that is the way it seemed. Then he asked me what brought me to Charlottesville, and I told him the truth — that we were there because we were expecting a few Warehouse members to come and party for the weekend. I wished I had something better than that to say, but — oh, well — I was a little nervous, and I am normally shy as it is. Then he said, "Oh, very cool." Next I asked if he wanted a drink or something, and he said no because he was expecting a wedding party and had to get inside shortly. I guess a friend of his had just got married. So then he turns and talks to a guy he knows that was sitting right by me, and Joey comes out of the bar, and he also could not believe it. I introduced him, and he was also keeping his cool. Then I waited very patiently for Dave to finish talking with the guy next to us, and I asked, "I hate to do this, but would it be okay to get a picture?" He said, "Oh, okay, sure — not a problem at all." So the guy next to us took our picture with Dave, and we shook Dave's hand one more time and said, "Thank you for being so kind." He said, "No problem at all. Anytime," and then he had to go inside.

So Joey and I sat down and had a beer or two outside. It was getting a tad chilly so we decided to go in also. It turned out that the only table left in the place was next to Dave's, so we took it, despite how bad that looked. We nodded, as did he, and we took our seats not even attempting to talk to Dave, as we thought that it would be too much, disrespectful. My thinking was that he was here in a bar with his friends and we didn't have time for attempting any kind of real or deep conversation. So we kept to ourselves for awhile. It was a tight fit in there, so I told Joey to move to the other side of the table, but he didn't so Dave's table had to slide over. I later told Dave, "I didn't mean you guys had to move. I didn't mean to appear rude." He said, "Oh, don't worry. I didn't think that at all." Then, a bit later, Dave turned to his friend and said very nicely, "This is Jeremy and his friend

Joey from the Warehouse." We said hello. Then, out of respect for his space, we didn't say much. After awhile, and another drink or two, somehow the Yankees came up in the conversation, and Dave said, "They are the only real team in baseball. They've been around forever" — or something to that effect — and we talked about that for a minute.

Shortly after that Dave raised his glass to us, and we did to him, and then they proceeded to go upstairs to the balcony of the bar, where they had a private party set up. Not too much later — around midnight, I guess — we decided to head back to our hotel; so we got up, looked up at the balcony, very casually said, "Dave," to get his attention, and waved goodbye. He gave us a peace sign and a thumbs-up, which we returned, and we walked out to get a cab.

—Jeremy Gilchrist

THE FINE LINE BETWEEN FAN AND "Psycho Stalker"

The most memorable day of my life is the day I met the one and only Dave Matthews. I had hoped and dreamed for so long that I would meet the man who is part of the most amazing band around, but I never thought I had a chance. I fantasized about meeting all of the band members, and I wondered what I would say if I did, how I would thank them for making such beautiful, incredible music. All my wildest fantasies became reality when I received a phone call from my friend who I was supposed to go to the Star Lake Amphitheater DMB concert with, in Pittsburgh, Pennsylvania, on June 3, 1999.

It was really late at night so I was surprised to hear the phone ring; I was in for an even bigger surprise when he told me that I was going to meet Dave Matthews the following week. I couldn't believe what I was hearing. It turns out that my friend was one of the five Warehouse members picked to attend the meet-and-greet at the Star Lake show. So this gave me a week to figure out exactly what I wanted to say to Dave. You'd think I would have come up with something by that time, but the day of the show came around and my mind was still completely blank. I wanted to express my deepest thanks to him for making such wonderful music, music that has changed my life in so many positive ways, but I also didn't want to seem like a pathetic, obsessive, psycho, stalking fan. I just wanted to have a normal conversation with him and not make him think I was about to burst into tears and throw myself on the ground and kiss his feet. But I hadn't thought of anything to say to Dave when the time came for me to meet him.

The whole experience was almost surreal. All of us were gathered backstage, and Dave just came out of nowhere, and I watched him in disbelief: it was so strange to realize that this was the Dave Matthews that I'd watched on stage and on TV and had listened to so many times before; now here he was shaking my hand and giving me a hug. I was incredibly nervous, but he was very warm and friendly, and he made me forget completely about how nervous I was. I was actually surprised at how calm and laid-back he was after seeing him act so crazy in concert. But it was only a few days after the infamous rib-breaking incident, and he must have been feeling pretty terrible. I really admired him for going out onstage and playing night after night while nursing his injury. We only had a few minutes with Dave—to chat, to get pictures and autographs. He came around to me and my friend.

The one particular thing that always comes to my mind when I reminisce about meeting Dave is the first thing he said to us. He made this obscure, hilarious comment about my friend's big baby-blue eyes—something like, "You'll get stopped at the border with those!" I have no idea what he meant, but it was hilarious to hear him make the comment. We ended up chatting about a few things; we asked him particularly about the song "#40." It had been making a strong comeback after disappearing for three and a half years from the set lists. Dave explained that he only remembers bits and pieces of the song—they had only played it a few times in 1995—which is why it has now been reduced to half its original length. We chatted about a few other things, then my friend and I expressed our deepest gratitude to Dave for doing the whole meet-and-greet thing, and Dave got set to leave. But before he left, I grabbed him and asked him to take one last picture with me since the flash on my camera hadn't worked when I tried to take a picture earlier. I borrowed my friend's camera and asked Dave if he would mind just one more little picture. He kindly obliged. As he put his arm around me I said to him, "Because I'll die if these pictures don't come out!" Oh, well. So much for not sounding like a psycho stalker.

—*Melissa Sandahl*

"WHEN YOU HAVE FUN, We Have Fun"

I didn't purchase tickets for a DMB show in my area this spring because I had a final scheduled the same evening. Just after lunch that day my friends called and said they had an extra ticket if I wanted to go. After thinking about it for less than two seconds, I shouted, "Of *course* I'll go!" We left five minutes later and went to a mall in the area before the arena opened. My friends went into a sporting-goods store, and I stood in the concourse complaining that we weren't tailgating in the parking lot like true fans. I looked up, and who was walking by? The braids in his hair poking out in all directions from an ill-fitting hat gave him away; why, it was none other than Boyd Tinsley, the violinist for DMB! Sheepishly, I said, "Boyd...?" He set down his J. Crew bags and immediately held out his hand while asking my name. After shaking hands we chatted for a few minutes, and I thanked him for the great concerts. He said, "When you have fun, we have fun." After he walked away, I sprinted into the store my friends were shopping in and dragged them out. They watched Boyd heading up the escalator, all the while wishing they hadn't been inside when he walked by. We went to the show and had an amazing time, as always. Since I never showed up for my Spanish exam I received an F. Was it worth it? Do you really have to ask?

—*Elis Good*

DAVE'S GRIPE WITH THE FANS

My friend Bill and I drove to New York City to see Dave and Tim play an acoustic concert at the Beacon Theater in the winter of '99. Before the show, however, we played an acoustic tribute to Dave and Tim at a party of Dave Matthews fans named "the Nancies." After we played we went to the show and then to the after-party, for which we had tickets. Dave was supposed to be there. He wasn't. He was next door greeting all these people in suits and tuxes, many of whom didn't even have any clue who he was. I, being a die-hard fan, was lividly pissed; so I decided to take matters into my own hands. Security was only letting dressed-up, artsy people in to where Dave was, so I grabbed some guy's sports coat (which he'd conveniently left at the bar), threw some beer in my hair, and flipped security my college ID. I got in! It was like going to see Santa Claus, but bigger.

When I finally got to meet Dave, he was a lot different than I thought. I didn't think he'd get very personal with me, but he did. I told him how sorry I was that he had to stand here and greet people like the pope. He laughed. I showed him my firedancer tattoo and I told him I liked how he broke up the chord structures in his songs. He said he was very appreciative that someone actually listened to his music, and he wasn't sure if he was going to continue touring acoustically, because of how rudely members of the crowd treated him and each other during the "intimate performances." Oddly enough, he asked me a question. He asked what I liked most about that evening's performance, if there were any highlights or any songs that stood out. I mentioned that I really appreciated his acoustic rendition of "The Stone," and he said it was also his favorite to play at the time. He said it was the only song characteristic of his old style of playing and that playing with the band brought a new dimension to writing songs. It was more of a collaborative effort now. I agreed. Then I shook his hand because there were more people waiting. In back of me there were two teenage girls crying their eyes out. Dave smiled and laughed a wicked laugh.

—*Erik Smith*

HOTEL VALET TIPS OFF FANS

June 11, 1999 is a day that I'll remember for years to come. The location was St. Louis, Missouri. It was the day that I met Dave Matthews, Boyd Tinsley, and Stefan Lessard. I know that people do not condone waiting outside a band's hotel, but I knew that if I did not meet Dave this time, I might never get the chance. So a friend and I went to the hotel at ten in the morning and waited—and waited, and waited. After only an hour had passed I had eaten all of the food and drank all the refreshments that I had brought. By two o'clock, hotel security had come to me twice and told me to leave, so I was thinking that what I was doing was wrong, and I was considering leaving, when a hotel valet guy ran up to me and said, "Hey, aren't you waiting for Dave Matthews?" I responded, "Yeah, but they're telling me that he isn't here and that I have to leave." This guy got the biggest smile on his face and said, "No, no, no. They tell everyone that. I am about to pull his car up right now. (Dave didn't actually drive it—it was his transportation to a radio show.) He'll be down in fifteen minutes."

After hearing this I was pumped! So we waited: fifteen minutes, thirty minutes—nothing. Then the doors open, and who walks out? Boyd Tinsley. He's reading a copy of *The Economist*, and he stops to say hi, take a picture, and sign my "DM BAND" Missouri license plates. A few minutes later the valet guy drives up, gets out, and winks at me. Not being the smartest fellow, I say, "What?" He kindly informs me that Dave is on his way down. Then the doors open and Dave walks out! Security tells me to get away, then Dave takes over. He tells them that it's okay and that we "aren't doing any harm." He kindly takes pictures, signs the plates, and tells me to enjoy the show that night. I was in shock. On our way back to my car, we were amazed to see Stefan. We had a short little conversation while he was signing and taking pictures. I asked him if the band planned to play "#40" that night, to which he jokingly responded, "what's '#40'? How can we play a song with no name?" Then he winked at me. As I walked away from the hotel that day, it still had not sunk in that I had just met Dave Matthews, Boyd Tinsley, and Stefan Lessard. I didn't believe it until I got the pictures back. Stefan had made a weird face in both our pictures.

—*Justin LaGrotta*

DMB FanFare Tip #2:

GET TO KNOW THE BUS DRIVER

I was bartending in Cleveland one hot summer night when one of my regulars came in for a drink. As we chatted, I learned that he was a stagehand, and we began discussing all of the bands he had done work for. My best friend and I were planning on going to a DMB show in a couple of weeks, and when I asked if he'd be there he said, "No, but my buddy drives Dave's bus. Try and find him and tell him you're a friend of mine." I was, like, "Yeah right. Like I'm really going to find the bus driver for DMB." Well, two weeks later my friend Corey and I were driving to Columbus, Ohio—which is a two-hour drive—partying and jamming and getting stoked for the show. We finally arrived at our hotel, and as we drove into the front area we saw a huge tour bus. Lo and behold, there was Dave, his face sticking out of the window, talking to a fan. As Corey went into the lobby to check in, I started to clean all the empty bottles and fast-food garbage out of the car. All of a sudden there was this guy next to me asking what I was doing. As fate would have it, it was the bus driver! When I told him that we had a mutual friend, we instantly hit it off, and the party officially began.

We spent the evening hanging out backstage and on the bus, meeting everyone and having a great time. They invited us to spend the next day with them because they had a day off. Of course, we did. They were all perfect gentlemen and a barrel of laughs. When we left to go home a few days later I wasn't sure if we'd ever see each other again or not. The driver and I continued to keep in touch, and when DMB came back through Cleveland a year later they gave us a call. Luckily they had a day off again, and so we were able to play. After a fun-filled day in Cleveland, we hung out in the hotel bar with Dave, Stefan, and Leroi. The whole time all I did was smile and laugh. I felt so comfortable with them, and I found them all, particularly Dave, to be very sincere. He's truly a very good guy, and I would've loved to have gotten to know him better.

We saw each other once more, four months later, and again it was a very special evening, filled with laughter and joy. Since then I've moved to Hawaii to go to school, and I haven't seen the band. I would love to run into Dave again one of these days, but if I never do, meeting him will always be one of the most memorable events of my life. Dave, if you're reading this, thank you for being who you are and for your incredible spirit. You are an inspiration to me as a fellow human being, and I hope to share good times with you again sometime in the future. Until then, aloha and God bless.

— Vicki Kopechek

A TRULY EMBARRASSING MOMENT
Some of my friends (Rachel Hershenberg, Jen Levy, Meredith Rosenberg, Jenny Kasen, Carah Linden, Jillian Denker, and Adam Mullinax) and I went to the Dave Matthews Band concert in Philadelphia in 1999. Well, two of my friends (Rachel and Meredith) flirted with some guys who gave them their backstage passes. It turned out that these guys were somehow affiliated with the band, and they gave my friends as many passes as they needed: eight. Well, after a *great* concert, the eight of us went backstage to see the band. We got in, and as we were walking down the hall, I tripped over a cart of food. As I was lying facedown on the floor, Dave Matthews walked out of his dressing room. The cart rammed into him, covering him in food! It was so embarrassing that I didn't want us to go in to see the band. Finally, my friends convinced me to go in — that Dave wouldn't know it was me. As we walked into the room where the band was everyone stopped talking, looked and pointed at me, and started to laugh! It was so embarrassing that I ran out of the room, missing my only chance, to date, to meet my favorite band.

— Shaun Kessler

ARMY UNIT
MARCHES TO DMB

Well, I'll try to make this as lively as I can. I want to express how much Dave and his band have had an impact on people. I am in the military, an Airborne Infantry unit. And every time we go to the field we look forward to coming home and relaxing and listening to Dave. We have an organized run here on post every couple of months. The units get in formation and we run four or five miles. While running, we have to sing cadences. My friends and I have turned DMB songs into cadences. Very untraditional! It is truly a funny sight to see. It's hard to imagine it or understand the humor unless you have some concept of how the army is. We get odd and unusual looks from other units and, of course, the general and his staff. We don't give a shit. Everyone in my unit, all thirty-two of us, is a DMB fan. Each one of us has a particular song that he can relate to. I've had a hard time, though, finding just one song to hold as a favorite. I haven't ever listened to a song from Dave that I don't like or hasn't touched me in some way. I hear so much truth in Dave's music. He has a remarkable gift to be able to make it sound like what he's singing about is the only thing he is thinking of at that time. All his emotion is in that song at that moment. I feel like I am in his mind, thinking the way he is, with every song. Not many artists can do that.

— Todd Metz

THE FEENEYS OF ATLANTA

My family and I have had two and a half years of outstanding Dave Matthews Band experiences, initiated by the first of the following letters. The story behind it all is simple. I faxed the first letter on January 20, 1997. Two days later Michael McDonald, DMB's tour manager, called me to apologize that he hadn't gotten back to me sooner, but that the band had been in Washington, DC, playing a little gig—Clinton's inauguration ceremonies! Michael said that Dave had read my letter and would love to meet us after the Dave and Tim show in Spartanburg, South Carolina, on February 8, 1997. The second letter takes liberties with DMB lyrics to describe our adventure at that show. We almost didn't make it backstage! I was thinking that other DMB fans may not get to hear too many stories from a forty-five-year-old father

MICHAEL MCDONALD, DMB TOUR MANAGER

The Feeneys, friend Nathan and Dave, 1997

describing the joy of watching his three children (and wife, too!) meet Dave Matthews and of beginning a two-and-a-half-year tradition of concerts (eight so far) and backstage visits. Since that night in Spartanburg, we've been to shows in Nashville, Tennessee; Greensboro and Raleigh, North Carolina; and here, in Atlanta, Georgia; as well as front-row-balcony seats for watching the MTV *Ten Spot* show. "The Feeneys of Atlanta," as we've come to be known, have enjoyed a unique relationship with Dave and the band's music.

John Feeney's Letters to Dave ...

January 20, 1997

Mr. Dave Matthews
The Dave Matthews Band
PO Box 1911
Charlottesville, VA 22903

Dear Dave:

I feel comfortable addressing this letter to "Dave" because I have listened to hour upon hour of Dave Matthews Band CDs. My three children have shown me the wisdom of your words and the wonderful magic of the Dave Matthews Band's music.

My oldest son, Kevin (eighteen), is a sophomore at the University of Georgia and has seen the band perform three times in the last year. Alison is fifteen years old and, along with Kevin, attended your Lakewood Amphitheater concert this past year in Atlanta. It was her birthday present — "The best gift I've ever had."

I am writing this letter, however, to tell you about my youngest son. Brian is ten years old and has developed a passion for music — *because of the Dave Matthews Band*. He has taken up saxophone lessons at school and has latched on to the guitar, as well. Every night, the last sound Brian hears before falling asleep is from one of his Dave Matthews CDs. We had to purchase three copies of your CDs so the kids could each have their own. Brian's favorites include the local *99X Acoustic Christmas* CD we got after waiting two hours in freezing December weather (and donating several of Brian's favorite, albeit too-small, winter coats to a local charity). He's constantly tinkering with the strings in an attempt to find the Dave Matthews magic. Brian's even developed your stage mannerisms and flying-feet style!

My wife and I do not have a musical bone in our bodies, so we're delighted that Brian has developed such a passion for music. His first concert was your show at Lakewood this summer in Atlanta. I sat (stood) with Brian throughout the concert, and it was wonderful to see and feel his excitement about you and the band. He was the first to recognize every song, and he sang along with each note. We ended up on the floor down in front for the last few songs — it was great!

Anyway, I'd like to thank you for your music — and for striking a chord in our young son's life that has uncovered a special feeling and passion. We're coming up to South Carolina for the February 8th show at the Spartanburg Auditorium. We'll be sitting up front, in the third row, seats C109 to C111. I'm sure you'll be hearing and seeing us throughout the concert.

If time is available after or before the show, I know Brian would be ecstatic to have the opportunity to meet you personally. Or, perhaps, if sometime during that show you have a chance to say hello to "Brian Feeney from Atlanta," you'd certainly make a young man feel the magic and make an old man very happy. Dave, I hope this letter reaches you during your travels around the East Coast. Kevin, Alison, Brian, and I look forward to seeing you in Spartanburg.

Sincerely,
John Feeney

February 10, 1997

Mr. Dave Matthews
The Dave Matthews Band
PO Box 1911
Charlottesville, VA 22903

Dear Dave:

There's *so much to say* since the Spartanburg concert. I hope I don't bore you, but *a thing or two I have to say here*. As the following story attests, we didn't think it was possible to *have a better time than most can dream*.

Our visit with you after the show was, as Brian would say, "awesome." Our journey that evening to meet with you was filled with a rollercoaster of anticipation, shock, despair, anger, hope, and, ultimately, triumph. So relax a bit, and, if you *care to share your time with me,* listen to a story of fulfillment *in a boy's dream, in a boy's dream....*

After the show (which was unbelievably good, by the way — particularly from the third-row-center seats we were fortunate enough to get), we all met at the front left of the stage and approached the stage entrance. During our phone conversation, Michael McDonald had instructed us to come to the front of the stage and tell them that "the guy who wrote the letter" was there and we'd be given access.

The beefy security guard at the door had other ideas, however. He informed us that without a backstage pass nobody would be let in. About that time, fifteen to twenty folks showed up at the same entrance with their preapproved yellow backstage passes and were admitted. I told the security guard the circumstances (in between a bevy — gaggle? — of giggling, pleading young ladies who wanted just to meet Dave) and said that Michael McDonald would surely let us in. *It's a typical situation* ... of miscommunication.

I started to sweat a little under the armpits as I looked at Diane, Brian, Alison, and Kevin. Their faith in me was still intact, but it was failing. The doubt and fear *thrown from the face of a child* can be piercing.

The security guard agreed to go backstage and pass the message to Michael. Ten minutes later he came back and said, "We've been advised that nobody is to be admitted without a backstage pass. Did he mail you any?" I said, "No! Michael McDonald just told me to come to this stage door!" "Sorry," he answered. "That's the rule. I can't make any exceptions."

It's at times like this that *you seek up an emotion, sometimes your well is dry.* I was drained emotionally, seeing a month of anticipation, excitement, and joy being crushed by an overzealous security guard with a heart of stone. I felt a wave of nausea *crash into me.* I was dumfounded. The kids were visibly upset and disappointed. Our night of excitement was coming crashing down upon us, and any credibility I had as a father was about to be shot. So I tried another tack.

I called to a stagehand and asked him to get a message to Michael McDonald. He said he would and left. *I was soon to be crazy,* as things got worse. *Here we have been standing for a long, long time.* Ten minutes later (now twenty to twenty-five minutes after the concert), the state police came down and said they had to clear the theater. *If you don't get in line, we'll lock you away.* So we were ushered to the lobby and outside. *Say goodbye* to any hopes of meeting Dave Matthews — and ever having your son believe in you again.

Our only consolation: maybe Dave hadn't left yet and we could see him head out to the bus in back. Brian was fighting back the tears. *I remember thinking sometimes we walk, sometimes we run away.* Well, we weren't going to run away from this without giving it our best shot. I looked at Brian and thought, *I let you down; let me pick you up.*

Let's give it a try, *and if nothing can be done, we'll make the best of what's around.* His eyes lit up with a flicker of hope, and we dashed down the front steps of the arena and headed for the backstage area. Alison, Kevin, and Brian literally flew to the back of the building, dancing the *two-step* past *dancing nancies, tripping billies* to get to the front of the gate area. I remember thinking, *what's the use in worrying, what's the use in hurrying?* It looks like this evening is not going to work out.

Boyd and Brian Feeney, 1998

A crowd of about two hundred or so fans was milling around the bus and stage entrance, hoping for a glimpse of Dave, who by now was almost surely gone. The fact that the crowd was still strong gave us *hope laid upon hope that this crowd will not subside,* for then all our efforts would have been for naught. Diane and I approached the security station by the bus, only to find the same security guard there! My first reaction was, this is *too much!* I guess there are just some things *we cannot change.*

Diane knew how much this meant to Brian and that at stake was any credibility I would ever have as a father. To relieve the tension and pent-up anger, she looked at me and said, *"Would you say you're feeling low and so a good idea would be to get it off your mind?"*

I could only laugh and say, *"I will go in this way and find my own way out."* She could sense the change in my tone and said, *"I'll back you up."*

Brian had run up to the fence next to the bus and squeezed his way to the front. The forlorn look on his face was only matched by the fear in my heart. *What would you say* to a young boy who was seeing his dream shattered? Oh, dear Brian, *it seems your eyes are troubled.* Bear with me, 'cause *whatever tears at us, whatever holds us down,* can be overcome with faith and commitment. *Let me climb you up to the top* of the fence so *I can see the view from up there, dreaming of things that we might have been.*

I reached into my pocket, thinking that a few bucks might change the security guard's mind — since *you pay for what you get.* Instead, I remembered I had a copy of the letter I had written to Dave. So I stuffed it into the security guard's hand and said, "Here — give this to Dave or Michael McDonald. Please. A boy's life depends on it." Upon his prompt return, with a wink and a nod, the security guard motioned us to the stage entrance. *We'll keep the big door open. Everyone'll come around.* Such sweet success! There are other times when *you seek up an emotion and your cup is overflowing.* Ours was overflowing with the relief of not failing *in a boy's dream.*

As you can see by the joy on the faces in our pictures (particularly Brian's), we did, indeed, make it to the top of the stairs. So now *celebrate we will, because life is short but sweet for certain.* And now I am the proudest father you've ever seen.

—*John Feeney*

TIM REYNOLDS RECRUITS FOR DMB

Well, this is more of a story about Tim Reynolds, who frequently plays with the Dave Matthews Band. I was in a music store in St. Louis, Missouri, just playing around on a Sammick acoustic guitar. While I was playing "So Much to Say," this short, wiry man plugged into an amp with a Gibson Les Paul Studio guitar. I started to hear high-pitched, twangy notes that overpowered my own guitar, but it sounded great. I stopped playing for a second, and then I started up again, playing "Ants Marching." The guitar in the background started playing this wild solo. I never saw anyone move his hands so quickly up the fret board. He made it look easy. I put the guitar I was playing down and approached the man. Before I said anything he asked me if I was a big Dave fan. I said, "As if it wasn't obvious," to which he replied, "Well, my name is Tim Reynolds. Perhaps you've heard of me." I almost fainted as I shook his hand, thinking that I was shaking the same hand that had graced many guitars on the road with Dave Matthews. We talked a little more — about guitar stuff, and Dave, of course. When he left it occurred to me that I hadn't asked him for his autograph. It didn't matter, though, because I will always remember what he told me. "If Dave ever breaks his wrist, I think I'll know where to turn: St. Louis."

— Greg Heinz

ONE GOOD TIM STORY
Deserves Another

Before moving out to California, I was a bass player in a Dallas band known as Baker Street. We had a studio in a small suburban commercial building, where we jammed on a nightly basis. It was there that I met Tim Reynolds, who at the time was playing (when available) for a band called Walter Mitty. One night we came in late for a jam session and passed a studio across the hallway that had the door cracked open. We started running through our set, and when it came time for a break we passed by that studio door again. We were stopped by the people inside — I remember one guy saying, "Hey, you guys are good. Who are your influences?" Without second thought I replied, "Dave Matthews." The guy at the door looked at us and said, "Cool. I like them, too. In fact, I'm friends with Dave." We were shocked upon hearing this. Within the next breath, Tim Reynolds was introducing himself and inviting us over to hang out. Unfortunately, shortly thereafter, Walter Mitty was no more, and I believe Tim left. It was at about that time that Dave and Tim started their tour and released their CD.

— *Scott Chambers*

AN ENTIRE DAY
SPENT WITH DAVE
Back in '96, me and a really cool guy named Matt Honeycutt were in charge of signing up comedians, bands, and lecturers to come to the college that I attended and he worked at: the Savannah College of Art and Design. We signed mainly small-time bands and comedians, and averaged about one show a week. Our program was really successful, though, and it caught the eye of the president of the college. He came to our office and asked us if we could sign up a big national act twice a year. He said he didn't want to make money; all we had to do was try to break even. Well, we went to work furiously, and before we knew it we had a contract sitting on our desk for Dave and Tim on February 13, 1997! We couldn't believe it. We had *no* idea what we had gotten ourselves into.

Pretty soon we had a radio spot playing, a ticket-sale date, and people calling us all day long trying to get front-row seats and backstage passes. Finally the day of the show arrived. We were at the theater at eight in the morning. The crew got there soon after and started setting up everything, which took nearly all morning. They were upset because they had broken Dave's stool the night before. They asked if we had one they could use; we scrounged one up and awaited Dave's approval. Dave and Tim finally got there around noon, and they immediately went to their dressing rooms. However, they came out after about fifteen minutes and met us. Dave tried out the new stool and said he liked it better than the last one because, "This one has more places to put my feet." He's pretty tall and very nice. Tim came out into the theater with a camcorder and started filming the architecture. He's really shy, and he didn't talk much. This was back when his head was shaved, and he had his fingernails painted black.

The caterer showed up, and we all ate together. There were about twelve people around the table, and Dave was the center of attention. He and Tim kept acting like they were gay and talking about how they wanted to go back to the dressing room and take a shower together. The tour manager finally told them they *had* to go sound check right then or it wouldn't get done. So we all went back out to the theater, and Dave and Tim went onstage for the sound check. They played for about forty-five minutes, although they only played one song: "Too Much." They spent the rest of the time making fun of each other and just farting around with the guitars. Then they went to their dressing rooms for about an hour. Dave came out first, and he just sat around with us. I sat on a couch with him for about three hours straight and just talked. He asked a lot about our school and about the different departments. He talked some about Marilyn Manson, who he thinks is "pretty funny." He also borrowed my walkie-talkie and started talking over the air like he was gay (much to Matt's chagrin). I wish I'd known his music as well as I do now, because now I have so many questions I wish I could ask him. Unfortunately, I was a newbie fan at the time. Anyway, when the show started I went out to my front-row-center seat and sat there for three hours, completely amazed. It could not had been *any* better. Several times during the show Dave looked down at me and smiled. I will never forget it.

After the show it was pretty hectic. I only got to go backstage for a second, and when I did there were two good-looking girls talking to Dave outside his dressing room, so I didn't want to bother him. I walked right by, and as I passed he looked up and brushed the girls off, asking me if I'd enjoyed the show. I told him I'd never forget it, and he seemed honestly pleased. He shook my hand, and that was that. We went on to sign Blues Traveler, Johnny Lang, the Wallflowers, and Tony Bennett while I worked for Matt, and I met all of them. No one could touch Dave — musically or personally.

—*C.J. Cowan*

Q+A WITH DAVE

Imagine picking up the phone, frantically dialing in an attempt to win a radio-station contest, and then actually winning. What did you win? A CD, a T-shirt, or — at best — concert tickets? Nope. You won the right to sit in a room with Dave Matthews for an hour while he answers questions and plays music! Plus, you get to bring a friend! Radio station WNEW (102.7 FM, New York) hosted Dave for an hour on March 24, 1999. When my friend and I met the WNEW staff at the designated spot the day after I won the contest, we still didn't know what we were getting into. We only knew that we were going somewhere and Dave was involved. The station people walked us and about twenty others to a bar down the block. When we entered we submitted questions that we could potentially ask Dave on the air, and then we took our seats. Right after Dave walked in my name was called, and I was told I would ask the second question on the air. Now, not only was I in a room with Dave, but I was also moved onto the tiny stage, literally four feet away from him. After the DJ asked two or three questions, Dave played a great version of "The Stone." Then, after a few more questions, it was my turn. I walked to the mike, asked Dave about his songwriting process, and then stood there as he answered my question. For a fan, it does not get much more personal than it was at that moment. Dave played three more songs that day: "Bartender — Don't Drink the Water," "Crash into Me," and "#41." I shook his hand at the end, and then he disappeared into a taxi (no limos for Dave, I guess!); he was on his way to tape VH-1 Storytellers.

I have seen nearly twenty Dave Matthews shows, but all those experiences pale in comparison to March 24, 1999. I felt as though I was in my living room and Dave was playing a private concert for my friends and family. When I next saw Dave, at Giants Stadium in May, I was only twenty rows back, but it felt like miles. Dave could have easily done the WNEW interview in a studio without any fans present. I cannot say enough good things about him for allowing us to be in the room while the interview was conducted and the songs were played. And I will always have the tape as proof that I met Dave Matthews!

—Brad Shafran

AN "ENTERTAINING" WAY
to Get Dave's Attention

Diagnosed with a full-blown case of DOS (Dave-obsession syndrome), I spend my free time writing—not letters to Dave, but extreme explicit sexual stories, first person, from me to him. As most Dave fans would probably agree, Dave is definitely sex-obsessed, so I figured this would be a way of getting his attention. After editing and reediting, I had a final draft of a sex story about myself and Dave. Pushing my way to the front of the crowd during a show, I threw the rolled-up pages (with my phone number) onto the stage. At the end of "Say Goodbye," Dave picked them up and put them in his pocket. The morning after the concert, I returned home from a friend's house to find a message from Dave on my answering machine! I nearly fainted. Not only did he say my name in the message, but he also said, "Thank you for the note, it was very entertaining!" I wonder how entertaining it really was for him. The time he called was something like four o'clock in the morning. At first I kicked myself for not having been home, but later I realized that no one would believe me if I said, "Yeah, guess what? Dave called me!" Now I am psyched, 'cause I have Dave Matthews talking to me on tape.

—*Kate Lapchick*

COP GETS
KISS FROM DAVE

I still shudder with excitement when I remember the day I met Dave Matthews! He and Tim Reynolds performed a concert in Columbia, South Carolina on April 13, 1999, at the Township Auditorium. I am a local police officer and a diehard fan of Dave's, so of course I almost died to hear that I was chosen as part of the security team for the event. I dreamily watched Dave and Tim perform. Most performers are usually out of the building in no time when the show is over, so I expected the same of Dave. But, to my surprise, a coworker told me that Dave was in the back signing autographs. I was so excited—I felt like a schoolgirl again! I rushed to the back and froze at the door. I couldn't go in. I was trembling. A guy with the event laughingly told me

50

that Dave was inside and I could go in. Well, I stepped through the door, and I didn't see him. The guy behind me laughed again and said, "He's behind the door." I went farther inside the room and there before me was Dave Matthews in person! I wanted to hug him and kiss him, but I had to remain "professional." I went up to him and we spoke. I told him my name, and we shook hands. There was so much noise around, so I didn't let his hand go; I pulled him towards me and whispered, "You are the most handsome man I have ever seen!" He looked at me and said, "Aww, you're so sweet," and he kissed me on my cheek. Needless to say, I almost fainted! I was on cloud nine for a week after that. I love you Dave!

—*Elaine McGee-Thomas*

DMB FanFare Tip #3:
WAITING PAYS OFF

I watched in amazement as my favorite musical artist of all time walked into the Canterbury Hotel lobby. Had it not been for my boyfriend, this opportunity would have walked right out the door with Dave Matthews himself. Instead, Paul

PAUL HENDRICKSON
Dave and Kelsey, 1999

reached out to shake the hand of this dream come true. "Great show tonight, Dave," Paul said. This unbelievable night began with an amazing show at Deer Creek Music Center in Indiana. "Lie in Our Graves" was absolutely phenomenal, then an encore of "Ants Marching" preceded the best night of my life. In the last few seconds of the show, Paul and I made a mad dash for his car and succeeded in escaping the frustrating postconcert traffic. We quickly headed for downtown Indianapolis, because Paul's sister, Laurie, had forked over two hundred dollars for a room at the exquisite Canterbury Hotel. Being the extraordinary fan that she is, Laurie knows that Dave always makes reservations at this hotel when staying in

Indianapolis. Paul and I approached the police outside the entrance. We were admitted as visitors due to the fact that Paul's sister had purchased a room. The lobby was quiet, despite the faint elevator music. We saw Laurie and a friend sitting on the green-velvet lobby couches. We quietly made our way over and joined them. Laurie leaned over and whispered to us, "Act like we're waiting for more friends to join us. The hotel will make us leave if they know we're here for Dave." Earlier, Laurie was told that Dave was in the bar, which is connected to the lobby. Only invitees could enter. And then the long—and I mean long—period of waiting began. It was now midnight, and we continued to wait in the lobby, receiving strange looks from the receptionists at the desk. Then the door to the bar opened. We all turned our heads, and out walked Boyd Tinsley. We congratulated him on his solo in "Lie in Our Graves," and we asked permission for a couple pictures. Wow, what a shock! We had just taken pictures with Boyd! But what we really wanted was to meet Dave. We waited, and waited, and waited. Sleepy-eyed, I looked at my watch. I panicked. It was almost one o'clock in the morning, and the parking garage we had parked in would shut down at one! Paul and I had to act fast. We exited the hotel as quietly as we had entered, but the second we hit the sidewalk we sprinted to the garage. Meeting Dave was on the line. We threw ourselves into Paul's blue Honda Accord and sped out of the garage. We were in such a frenzied hurry that we drove the wrong way down a one-way street. We parked alongside the curb, ran back to the hotel, and quietly reentered the lobby. Laurie informed us that we hadn't missed Dave. The wait continued until two o'clock in the morning. All our eyes were fixed on the bar door when it slowly, but surely, opened, and out walked Dave. Paul stood up and reached out his hand, "Great show tonight, Dave," he said. I was at a loss for words and just watched. "Thanks, man," Dave replied. "We'll try and mix it up a little for you tomorrow night." (There was another show the next night, on June 22, 1999.) He signed some CDs we'd brought with us, then we all took our turn for a picture with Dave. I walked up to him, smiled, and hugged him for the camera. I never wanted to let go!

—*Kelsey Gilreath*

A HIGH SPEED CHASE
with the DMB Tour Bus

I'm someone who is usually very quiet and reserved, so the night of January 22, 1999 was quite an experience. After a long day of cutting classes and driving to get to the Bloomsburg, Pennsylvania, performance of Dave Matthews and Tim Reynolds, my friend Miguel and I shared the most exciting night of our lives. When the amazing twenty-four-song set was over our adrenaline was hitting the roof, and we sprinted around to the back of the auditorium to see Dave board his bus and possibly have an experience that we could brag about the next Monday at school. We waited about an hour or so in the dead cold, and Dave finally came out, waved to the crowd, and boarded his bus. This only added to our excitement.

When the bus began to drive through the parking lot, Miguel and I chased it on foot. In a sudden burst of insanity, Miguel caught up with the bus, ran around the front, and stood in its path, forcing it to stop. Then I caught up, and I could not believe my eyes. Miguel was standing in front of the bus, waving, with a huge smile on his face. What was more exciting was that Dave was waving back through the window of the bus. Needless to say, this provoked even more excitement in me, and I joined Miguel at the front of the bus, waving insanely. Dave looked at me, laughed, and waved back. Miguel and I jumped up and down and hugged each other like idiots while Dave watched. The experience, however, did not end there.

With an even larger adrenaline rush, Miguel and I sprinted to my car with the hope of following Dave to his hotel, where we could meet him. As we followed the bus, we thought that we would try to see if we could get more acknowledgment from Dave Matthews. So, with "Warehouse" blasting from the open windows of my car, we pulled up beside the bus and danced and screamed out of the windows. Possibly seeing us as a threat, the bus suddenly kicked into high gear and hit high speeds; we found ourselves chasing the bus, which was weaving through traffic and traveling at speeds that were almost impossible to keep up with. After about an hour we finally lost the race. Dave got away and we found ourselves lost in the middle of the night and in the middle of nowhere. After making a phone call to my mother, who was not as excited as we were about our experience, we checked ourselves into a hotel for the night. Needless to say, we had that story to tell at school on Monday.

— Timothy Harden

A TOUR BUS STORY
with a Happier Ending

My friends and I saw Dave and Tim at the Township Auditorium in Columbia, South Carolina, on the '99 tour. It was a great show, and we decided to wait outside for them and try to meet them when they came out. Well, I would say about a quarter of the audience had the same idea. We were unlucky—it was the road manager's wife's birthday or something, so they stayed inside and celebrated for a long time while we waited outside in the cold. Finally, they came out, and Dave was nice enough to sign some autographs, but he left before my friends and I could get ours. Unsatisfied, we decided to follow his tour bus to his hotel. Little did we know his hotel was in Greenville—the next night's show was at Furman University. It was a two-hour drive, but we didn't care. We were gonna meet Dave. There was one problem, though. We were running out of gas.

We decided to drive ahead of the bus and get gas, and that way we could watch it pass and be on the road in time. Well, of course, that didn't work, because all of the gas stations were closed, and we lost the bus. We were also lost, and we didn't know what exit to take. We decided to take a random exit, get gas, and call it a night. We got off at an exit and stopped at a red light. My friend Ross asked, "What is that ahead?" "Holy shit!" we yelled. "It's the tour bus!" We were thrilled. We went over to it and there was Dave. He said that it was too cold outside for autographs and told us to come inside the bus. So we went inside and met Dave Matthews! It was awesome. He was really cool, and he signed our autographs. He kept thanking us for coming, which was surprising, because we knew he must have thought we were psychos for following his tour bus. He didn't seem to mind, though. It was great. After we got off the bus and he couldn't see us anymore, we started jumping around and hugging each other like young schoolgirls. We are all huge fans, and it meant so much to us that Dave took the time out and made us feel so good. Thanks a lot, Dave! Our next goal is to meet the rest of the band. I hope we won't have to go to such weird lengths to do so.

—Brendon Vallee

THE BACKSTAGE QUEEN

At this point I have been to fifteen Dave Matthews Band concerts, and I have gotten backstage at eleven shows. Some of my stories about acquiring backstage passes are just as exciting and unbelievable as my encounters with band members. I have met all the members of the band numerous times, except for Stefan. I have not been lucky enough to meet him yet. I am only going to share two of my most original stories.

The first time I received a backstage pass was on May 29, 1998, in Bonner Springs, Kansas. I was literally standing in the right place at the right time. I was just loitering around the gate, watching the few lucky souls with passes. I saw a man and woman go back, and two minutes later they came out again. I walked up to them and asked general questions about the events behind the gate. The man insisted that there was nothing going on. He said no band members came out and it was basically a bunch of people sitting around. He said he was just going to leave because nothing was happening. I asked if I could have his pass, and he said, "Sure, but it's pretty boring

 back there." He peeled off his pass and just handed it to me. So, there I stood with a backstage pass. I assumed I could just walk back with the pass, but as I approached the gate the burly local security guard stopped me. He

Della, Leroi, and Della's friend Natalie,1999

asked if I was on the list. I had no clue what he was talking about, and so I just told him that if I had a pass then I must be on the list. This must have been an acceptable response because he opened the gate and let me through. Now I was behind the gate, but without an escort. I had no idea where to go. All I could see was a bunch of crew members loading the trucks. I wandered around for a few minutes and found the other people. I started to small talk with random fans, and ten minutes later Dave came out. He immediately started chatting with what looked like some important people. I was amazed at my luck. Fifteen minutes earlier I had just been waiting, hoping to get a glimpse of a band member, and now I was within ten feet of Dave Matthews. Dave hobnobbed with the important people for a few minutes, occasionally glancing at the small group of fans that I stood with. When their conversation was finished, Dave turned and approached the fans. As I was ransacking my brain for something to say, Dave walked straight up to me and said, "You have beautiful eyes." I was dumbfounded, but somehow I got the composure to thank him for the compliment. I then proceeded to talk to Dave about various things, including what a great idea it was for him to wear a sweater and all black for an outdoor summer concert in Kansas. After I talked with Dave for ten minutes about athletes, sweat, and sweaty athletes, he moved on to talk to other fans. I decided to stick around and see if I could get his autograph. In fifteen minutes he returned, and I spoke with him at length about Chicago, which I gathered was one of his favorite cities.

On May 15,1999, I was in Detroit, Michigan, to see a series of Dave Matthews Band shows. At a previous concert my friend and I had met up with the opening band, Corey Harris and the 5 X 5. To make an incredibly long story short, the opening band offered us passes and asked us to come to the Palace (the venue) a few hours before the show. We did go to the show early, but when we attempted to pick up our backstage passes we found that the box office was closed and would not open for at least an hour. As we walked back to our car, we saw Corey Harris talking to some fans outside. We explained our problem to him and he said we could just walk back with him (he being one of the performing artists and all). So, that's what we did. When I stepped through the back entrance I saw a group of crew members taking a break, and I heard a Dave Matthews Band song blasting on the intercom. I remember thinking how annoying this must be for the band. I pictured the band members trying to relax in their dressing rooms and being forced to listen to themselves on the intercom every day. As I followed Corey around backstage, I had an opportunity to peer into the venue. I could see thousands of empty seats under the flashing stage lights. At that moment I realized that I was not listening to the Dave Matthews Band on an intercom system. They were actually playing onstage! My friend and I were allowed into the venue, and we got to see our own private Dave Matthews Band concert from the front row! We watched, and of course we danced, as the Dave Matthews Band performed with Jamal Millner (of the 5 X 5), who later played at that evening's concert. After sound check, we got to hang out backstage, where I met Leroi Moore. I also got another chance to talk to Dave Matthews, right before he announced the opening band, and I went to my seat to enjoy another incredible concert.

—Della Moran

ODE TO CARTER
I've always known that DMB was full of amazing musicians, but I never really knew their full extent until I saw them live in Houston, Texas, in July of 1999. Let's take Carter Beauford, for example. During one of the numbers, Carter decided to change around his set a bit and began to do it *right in the middle of the song!* He put one of his drumsticks in his mouth and continued going crazy with his other hand as normal. Here's the amazing part: the sound never changed! He was picking up drums and switching one out and moving them around and all the while the drum part of the song never changed. It's, like, sure he can do it with one hand, but it's even easier with two!

—Spencer Oscarson

DMB SPIRITUALITY
Although I have had some interesting experiences while following the Dave Matthews Band for more than five years, I would like to describe an experience that I had in Virginia Beach, Virginia, while attending a DMB concert. My fiancée, Kelly, and I drove there from Georgia to see the band play in the summer of '97. The concert, as all of Dave's have been, was amazing. However, the most amazing aspect of this particular concert was the "vibe," if I may call it that, or the emotions that ensued because of the band's music. I cannot put the emotions that transpired between Kelly and me into words, but the power and the emotions that the band put forth in their music had a interesting effect on us. Proverbial and typical as it may sound, the music and emotions

of the Dave Matthews Band took us, together, to an alternate mental and emotional land. For about two hours the music served as a vehicle for Kelly and me, taking us to an emotional world that only music can describe. It is difficult to explain; however, I can say that the music of the Dave Matthews Band lifted us to a higher emotional and spiritual level. For those two hours we were no longer in Virginia, the United States, or the world. For a short time we were inhabitants of a flawless musical land, courtesy of the Dave Matthews Band. Only a band with such a powerful and hypnotic sound could produce feelings and emotions like these. Thank you, guys. You will never know how much you have affected my life.

— *David Thomas*

"IS THAT THE GIRL DAVE KISSED?"

On May 29, 1998 I went to the World Music Theater in Tinley Park, south of Chicago, to see the Dave Matthews Band. I wasn't expecting anything more than an amazing concert. The day began just like any normal concert day; I was excited when I first opened my eyes. Of course, I was extremely impatient to get to the concert early, so my friends and I ended up being the first people waiting outside the gate, at around four in the afternoon. I remember listening to the sound check. They were playing "Stay (Wasting Time)" with the female vocalists from Poi Dog Pondering. After hearing that I was extremely excited for the show. The gate opened, and I sprinted in with our blanket to get lawn seats in the front center: that was my goal. We had second row the year before, so I was a little disappointed with the seats we got, but I knew that I wouldn't be as soon as the boys went on stage.

At about five o'clock we were waiting for Poi Dog to begin. A few of my friends and I left the lawn for awhile to check out the parking-lot area and buy T-shirts. We ran into some people we knew and chatted for awhile. I wasn't really paying attention, until one of my friends said, "Hey, you guys! Look over there — it's Dave!" I was like, "Yeah, right. Whatever." Of course I looked anyway, and then I realized that my friend was completely serious. Dave Matthews was standing in an XRT booth being interviewed. We ran over to watch.

Nobody else really noticed that Dave was right there for a couple minutes, so that gave me the opportunity to stand about five feet from him. Immediately, I felt something taking over my body. I could hardly stand still. I was shaking from complete shock. I knew exactly what was going on — I just couldn't believe it. I felt as though I was the only person standing there, surreal-like. Tears filled my eyes, and then I noticed that Dave's eyes were looking right into mine. I just kept staring. I couldn't do much else. My friends and I watched the interview until it was over. By the time Dave signed off, I had calmed down a bit. I looked around me, and there were people everywhere, but I hadn't noticed any of them until then. Dave began to make his way out of the XRT booth. I assumed that he would immediately go backstage, but he didn't. I couldn't really see where he was walking, but one of my friends said, "Heather, he's coming over to you." I just stood there in the middle of the huge crowd of people. Then I saw Dave walking towards me, shaking people's hands. I looked up and there he was, right in front of me — but no, I couldn't say anything. He looked at my friends and said, "What's her name?" They yelled, "It's Heather!" Dave looked me in the eyes, gave me a hug and a kiss on my cheek, and said, "Nice to meet you, Heather." In my left hand I was carrying my new '98 spring tour T-shirt, and I reached out to hug Dave with my right hand. I guess you could say that I blacked out a little bit. After he left I buried my head in my friend's chest.

Okay, so that made my night, not to mention all the attention I got afterwards. I kept hearing people whisper to each other, "Is that the girl Dave kissed?" Every time I heard that it put a huge grin on my face. My friends and I went back to our lawn seats to listen to Poi Dog play. The entire time I just sat there smiling, thinking about what had happened, trying to figure out if it really did happen. Then Dave and the boys came onstage and opened with "Don't Drink the Water." The crowd was wild already. I listened, sang, and danced my heart out. About halfway through the show, Dave started talking. His exact words were, "There's a little tiny person out there, Heather, with a lovely tear in her eye, and this song's for little Heather." They played "#41." At the time I couldn't really make out exactly what Dave said, but I was sure I heard my name. I was lucky enough to receive a tape of the show.

— *Heather McCarthy*

DAVE MATTHEWS:
Honorary Crew Member
My girlfriend and I left New Orleans on May 4, 1999 and headed for Mobile, Alabama, to see Dave and the band perform live. Well, the concert was better than we ever could have imagined it would be. And although we enjoyed the concert immensely, the walk back to our car is something that we won't soon forget, for it was then that we discovered something truly extraordinary about Dave. On the way back to our car, we saw the tour buses and about fifty people waiting outside of the barricades to get a glimpse of the poetic master, so we figured what the hell and wedged our way up to the front to get a closer look. Then, one by one, the band members boarded the bus: first Carter, then Leroi, then Boyd, then Dave. (Stefan came out also, but he went his separate way to his own bus.)

The crowd began to cheer and chant in unison the name of each member, which inevitably encouraged them all (yes—even Dave!) to walk up to the front of the bus and wave at all of the adoring fans. But the most exciting part was yet to come. Assisted by his bodyguard and manager, Dave exited the bus, walked right up to the barricades, and graciously passed in front of his screaming and hysterical fans to shake hands and greet us all. He then reboarded the bus to wait for its departure, which seemed to be taking a really long time.

At this point he did the most amazing thing! Dave Matthews himself walked off the bus, went back into the arena, and began to help the stagehands and crew members to break down the staging and lighting for the sold-out concert he had been the star of only two hours earlier. He may have been bored or just ready to leave, but all of the diehard fans who were still around to witness this rarity were truly impressed with the coolness and unpretentiousness of Dave Matthews, and no matter how highly we thought of him prior to that moment, our opinion of him increased overwhelmingly upon witnessing that very down-to-earth moment. Way to stay grounded, Dave! We love ya!

—*Michael Delsa*

A GENEROUS GESTURE

Where to begin? Where to begin? I suppose by telling you my name — Mark — and where I work — the House of the Good Shepherd. The House is a nonprofit organization that caters to the needs of emotionally and mentally challenged children in Utica, New York. The majority of these children come from broken homes, if any home at all. I'm employed as a crisis-intervention specialist at the school there. One day I was in my office with one of the residents when a friend of mine stopped by to drop off tickets to an upcoming Dave and Tim show at the Stanley Theater, which is located in downtown Utica. Upon learning what the tickets were for, the child became elated, stating how lucky I was and that he'd probably never get to go to a concert.

That night I went home with that child's words ringing in my head. I decided to write Dave and Tim a letter telling them a little about the kids, hoping to persuade them to stop by and say hello. Given the magnitude of Dave's celebrity I really didn't think I'd get a response, but it couldn't hurt to try. If he did actually get the letter, who knows? Dave seemed like a real salt-of-the-earth kind of guy. So I sent it out one cold day just prior to our Christmas break.

The vacation flew by, as vacations always seem to do, and I found myself back behind my desk in what seemed like a blink of an eye. It was about midday when I finally got an opportunity to check my voice mail. I was listening, deleting, listening, deleting, when I got this message from a guy saying that Dave had read my letter and wanted to set something up for the kids. At first I thought it was someone busting my chops, but there weren't many who knew about the letter besides my girlfriend, the office secretary, and my brother, who also works at the House. So I wrote down the number and looked up the area code in the phone book: lo and behold, it was a Virginia area code. Nah — can't be. Could he have actually gotten the letter?

I dialed up the number and this woman answers, "Red Light Management. Can I help you?" I, with my ever-so-cool demeanor, hung up on her. Then I sat back, gathered my thoughts, and dialed the number again. The same woman answered. This time, of course, I stayed on the line and asked for the gentleman who had left the message. Next thing I knew I was talking to this guy, and he told me that Dave had a real soft spot for kids and would like to set something up. He told me he'd be in touch to finalize the plans the week prior to the show. I hung up the phone and sat there in this strange fog of amazement, speechless.

Well, needless to say, the weeks prior to the show didn't pass quite as quickly as my vacation had. But finally I was back on the phone with the gentleman from Red Light, who gave me the number of Dave's tour manager, Mike, and told me when I should call. I called Mike the day before the show and finalized everything. The day of the show we loaded all the kids on rented school buses and headed to the Stanley Theater, where Dave and Tim put on an excellent concert. The kids had the time of their lives — singing, dancing, and laughing. I have to admit the whole thing made me a bit misty-eyed. They played "Don't Drink the Water," "So Much to Say," "Too Much," Lyle Lovett's "If I Had a Boat," "Dancing Nancies," and they closed with "Satellite." It was a night the kids would not soon forget — and believe me, they still haven't.

My only regret of the evening (as if I could actually have any) would be the fact that the child I initially wrote the letter about couldn't attend and that I didn't shake Dave's and Tim's hands and thank them personally. Not that I wasn't afforded the opportunity — I guess I just got a little shy at the prospect. So, Dave, Tim, if by chance you read this, sorry, and thanks again for providing the children with a most memorable evening.

— *Mark Pauley*

"A WONDERFULLY NICE MAN"

During the Dave Matthews and Tim Reynolds tour my cousin's friend in Indiana became ill with cancer. Her friend was the all-out greatest Dave Matthews fan. Her illness was terminal and she wanted only one thing: to meet and hear Dave Matthews. Dave had heard about her story through an e-mail he received. A few days later my cousin was going up to her hospital room to visit her friend, and she heard that her friend was listening to — of course — Dave Matthews. However, when she entered the room she saw Dave Matthews himself singing and playing for her friend. I couldn't believe it when I heard it. But what a wonderfully nice man he must be to do something that special for one of his fans. Thank you, Dave.

—Joshua Hancock

DREAMS COME TRUE
for Those Who Try... Dave Matthews was set to

finish his 1999 summer concert tour with two shows at the Meadows Amphitheater in Hartford, Connecticut, on August 6th and 7th. By the time word reached me, both shows had already sold out. I had wanted to buy tickets for this girl, Steph, as a birthday present. The point of her very life was to meet (and marry) Dave Matthews. Despite this triviality, I was keen on her, but tickets were not available for either show. Fate works in mysterious ways. I was toiling through my ratrace of a job when I received word: they were adding a third show on Sunday the 8th! Tickets went on sale, and I bought lawn seats. To make sure Steph was available, I had to tell her about the tickets. So I had my gift, but it wasn't a surprise. The surprise came later, in early July. Connecticut's 104.1 FM had a contest called "Camp Matthews." If you won, you would not only receive tickets to one of the first two sold-out shows, but also a spot at a secret campsite with transportation to and from the show. Guess what? I was caller number twenty! I won tickets for Friday the 6th! Steph, of course, was not to know. I e-mailed her saying she had to show up at the campsite on Friday afternoon, no questions asked. I gave her directions. So the stage was set. The actors were prepped. I arrived at the secret locale to set up camp. Steph arrived half an hour later. Then we got on the 7:30 bus and went to the show. Was Steph psyched? A little. No, I'm kidding — I mean a lot. The band played mostly slow stuff, which was understandable since they had to play three shows in as many days, but the band members themselves were quite energetic. It was a good beginning for a memorable weekend.

The next day we had to decide what we were going to do that night without Dave Matthews tickets. A plan was born. I had been given Steve Miller tickets the week before by my friend Rick, but I wasn't able to attend the show. The tickets were unused. Steph once had a friend who accidentally used Lollapalooza tickets for the H.O.R.D.E. tour (or vice versa). Was it possible that the same thing could happen for us? We had to try. Let's all thank Steph for having friends: we got in! We passed the first gate, where they just make sure you have tickets by having you hold them up in the air. Covering "Steve Miller" with my thumb, I left "Band" visible for security to see. We were then funneled into the ticket-taking line, where the lax security guard ripped the tickets and let us in. Ha! Then, with Steph working her magical charms on one fifteen-year-old security guy and using our ticket stubs from the night before, we were able to get past lawn seating and dance in the aisles about thirty yards from Dave. Cool.

Sunday's tickets were for a patch of sod so distant from the stage that you could watch what was happening on one of three television screens provided. I would like to tell you right now how Steph and I ended up with seventh-row seats, but I'm afraid some secrets are better left untold. We found our way to seats in the seventh row. When the owners of those seats showed up, we moved to the sixth row. This is when things grew interesting. The show began and for the first two songs no one appeared to claim our seats. Then the women with beer came. They had a beer in each hand and stopped directly in front of me. The short blonde one looked at me and said, "Would you mind if we stood in front of your seats if we give you this beer?" Sure! Why not? It turns out that her dad had our seats two nights before, and they used the ticket stubs to get in. They figured they'd be able to get her dad's old seats if they bribed with beer. Good idea. Too bad they ran into us scroungers. Too bad the actual owners of the seats arrived with a six-foot-something "usher" a couple of minutes later. Shit. The security guy looked at the beer girls' tickets and thought they were good. He didn't notice the date. Then he asked for our tickets. I dug into my pocket as if I had something in there besides lint. Nope. I kept digging. I looked the guy squarely in the eyes and said, "I can't find them." He asked me if these were my seats. I told him, "Yeah. I mean no. But we just wanted to jam, man." As he reached for my neck, Steph made her move. She told the guy to recheck the beer girls' tickets. It was kill or be killed, right? And mine was the first neck on the chopping block. He turned to the girls and started to push them out of the row. Over his shoulder he said, "And you two get back to your seats." Right, Sir. I felt bad for the girls. I mean, after all, we kept their beer. But I put mine down underneath our new, seventeenth-row seats in observance of my guilt. Steph drank hers. And then she drank mine. She needed as much courage as possible for what she would try to pull off at the end of the night: meeting Dave Matthews.

The show was good. Good enough to cause another night of rioting by drunken middle-class white kids from Connecticut. At the end of the set Steph and I were separated. She began her attempt at glory, and I lay back to enjoy the encore. Once the concert was over, security tried to make everyone leave. I procrastinated as much as possible, but as I was being escorted out of the amphitheater I noticed Steph heading into the meet-and-greet backstage area. She got in! With the grace of God, Steph went into foreign territory, and for me began the long trip back to the parking lot, where I'd decide what I was going to do. The decision didn't take too long. I'd wait. And boy, did I wait. After watching kids suck down nitrous balloons in front of me forever, I finally fell asleep in my car. At 1:45 in the morning Steph was pleasantly surprised to find that she still had a ride home. Wait—did I say "pleasantly"? I meant "psychotically." That's the best word for it. Ya see, she met Dave. Yup, that's right. *She met Dave!* I saw her among a group of five other people coming into the parking lot. She ran up to the car.

STEPH: Do you know who the Platters are?
ME: You mean the band?
S: Yeah. That's Les. He was the guitarist for the Platters.
M: (to Les): Hey. What's up?
S: Do you notice anything different?
M: Uhhhhhhhhhhhhhh...
S: I only have one ring. And do you know why?
M: Uhhhhhhhhhhhhhh...
S: *It's 'cause I met Dave!*

She had two rings on a chain around her neck earlier in the night. One was hers and the other was for Dave, if she met him. She met him. He now has a ring. In a way, in her mind, they're married. Les, the guitarist for the Platters, had taken his daughter and her friends backstage to meet Dave. Using her cosmic powers across the barrier of the meet-and-greet wall, Steph had manipulated this man into taking her with them. She met Dave. Dave signed her shirt, Steph gave him the ring, and Steph almost broke into a seizure. She took a drag from Dave's cigarette, and do you know what? She hates smoking! Incredible. The whole thing was incredible.

Fortunately, Les had parked his car in the same lot as mine, and they all walked back together. Steph and I drove back, her giddy and me tired. I went to work heavy-eyed the next morning, but I had a story no one could take away from me. Dreams come true for those who try, and adventures are guaranteed to those who follow the dreamer.

—Alex Effgen

DMB FanFare Tip #4:
ACT LIKE YOU BELONG BACKSTAGE – Even if You Don't

The Dave Matthews Band did a show in Montreal, Quebec, on May 2, 1998, and my sister and I drove all the way from New Jersey to see the band for the fortieth time. We stopped at the Canadian border, where our car was searched, and then we found we were almost there. As we were trying to figure out how to get to the arena we realized that we were driving behind the band's tour bus. We decided to see how far we could get, so we followed the bus in, parked right near it, hung out, and waited for the band. Boyd and Stefan got off, gave us a friendly wave and a hello, and walked inside. I was standing by a door, and I just figured I would try and open it. It wasn't locked so we walked inside and acted like we should be there. The band was sound checking. We got to hear a few songs and have something to eat. People were looking at us a little funny, but we just acted like we should be there. Stefan's wife and their newborn baby, Diggy, walked in. She was really nice, and the baby was adorable. Then people started to get a little more suspicious, and finally someone from the crew came up to us and said we couldn't be here. He was really nice about it, and we at least got a chance to hear sound check and meet Diggy. The show was amazing, as usual, and it was definitely worth the long trip to Canada.

—Stacey Borelli

NEVER UNDERESTIMATE
the Acoustics of an Arena
The lights had just died in the First Union Center, and "Crush" ended abruptly. My first Dave concert, November 30, 1998, in Philadelphia, was the most magical experience I've ever had. My friends Stacie and Meg were giggling like the schoolgirls we all were, just tickled pink to be in the same room as Dave Matthews himself. Dave thanked the audience and adjusted his guitar strap, looking dazedly at the crowd as it grew more and more silent. "How close do you think we are to Dave?" I asked Stacie. We were sitting in the sixth row, off the floor, to the right of the stage. "I don't know." "Close enough to scream, Stace?" Before Meg and Stacie could voice any objections, I screamed with my full voice, "I love you!" Dave cocked his head to the side and glanced over at section 101 where I was jumping wildly in the sixth row. "I guess someone loves me here," he said, smiling. He had that right: someone loved him.

—Jen Nagel

"MR. CARTER BEAUFORD
ON THE DRUMS"
This past August I was set to go back to Radford University. But before I left a few buddies of mine wanted to go to Charlottesville, Virginia, for the day. So, Dana, Matt C., Ryan, Ellenwood, and myself went up there. As my last day with my friends was winding down, they decided to stop at Harris Teeter (a supermarket) and grab some refreshments for the ride back to Virginia Beach. While I was waiting in the parking lot I saw a huge black Navigator pull up and park. Thinking nothing of it, I looked at the driver, and he looked very familiar to me — not familiar like I knew him, but familiar like I'd seen his face before. So I decided what the hell. I walked up to the car and tapped on the driver's side window. As he rolled down the window I asked him if he was Carter Beauford. He said he was, and I picked my jaw up off the ground and tried to get a coherent sentence out. I began to explain how great DMB is and how wonderful it is to be at the shows. I also threw in the fact that he amazes a lot of people behind those drums. Now, I wanted proof that I had met "Mr. Carter Beauford on the drums." Realizing that

asking for two autographs might be pushing my luck, I felt the unselfish need to get one for my good friend Chris (who was unable to make the trip). Carter is his drumming idol, so I told Carter about Chris and how much he practices "Two Step" to get it just right. To make a long story even longer, Carter wrote the autograph out to Chris and told him to "keep jammin'." I felt that since I had the honor of meeting my friend's hero the least I could do was get a signature for him. So that's my story, and I'm sticking to it.

—*Jeff Lewis*

STEFAN, Alone on the DMB Bus

The trip began in Jersey. We trekked on down to Roanoke, Virginia, for the first show of the 1998 tour. My girlfriend (now my fiancée) and I had seen Dave and the boys plenty of times before this, but we'd never seen them in Virginia, and we'd never seen a first show. We arrived in Roanoke the day before the show. We scouted the place. We were driving alongside Victory Stadium, where the boys would be playing, while they were doing the sound check. It was great! Finally, after a night of hanging around and doing things that probably can't be mentioned in this book, morning arrived. Entering a stadium on a general-admission ticket is sometimes not fun, but we got a great spot. The show was incredible! It was great hearing new DMB songs that would later burn a hole through my speakers from playing them so much. The next day we got on the road and were Jersey bound. Driving past the Hotel Roanoke, I saw a tour bus that looked like Dave's. We took a detour down to the parking lot of the hotel. There were about two other people waiting by the bus. We sat around for a few minutes and out came Stefan. We jumped out of the car, walked— okay, ran—over to him and asked him to take a picture with us. He was very down-to-earth. We took the picture, and we also got him to sign a couple of things. I was a little disappointed when I asked him if anyone else would be coming out and learned that he had the entire bus to himself. He said that everyone else had gone up to C'ville the night before. Not a problem —I don't want to be the person who asks for too much. Well, after that the weekend was at an end. We drove home and were very happy. I got to meet one of the guys who changed my life with music.

—*Mike Hayes*

"AM I REALLY THAT SUCKY?"

The countdown to the concert was finally over, and I was there. The excitement in my stomach was taking over my whole body, and the energy was overwhelming. It was Dave and Tim, and they were giving a small private concert. I was waiting in line to get in when I saw a good friend who I hadn't seen in awhile. I started bragging to him about how I had eleventh-row seats, only to hear that he had second-row seats. I can't even describe the jealousy I felt, and I knew for sure that I wanted to see Dave up close more than he did. I wanted those tickets. I knew I wasn't going to get his seats, but he did tell me that he would let me and my friend sit with him until somebody made us go back to our real seats. Surprisingly enough, they started the concert and nobody made us move. Dave and Tim worked their magic. They had gotten to the end of the third song when the real owners of the seats came. We got up and started to walk to our seats; I was so pissed off because I didn't want to go back so many rows. Then I heard, "Am I really that sucky?" It didn't click right away, but Dave was talking to me! I started freaking out. Tears filled my eyes. The love of my life was talking to *me!* I started repeating over and over again, "No, no, I love you. I wouldn't be moving if I didn't have to." He put his hands over his heart and started to play again. We ended up having to go back to our real seats, but the concert was awesome, and I'll never forget it. Dave, if you're out there, you will never suck, no matter what you do. Thank you for bringing many smiles to my face every day.

—*Sophie Boddington*

THE POWER OF DMB

I truly discovered DMB while I was living in Amsterdam during the winter of 1998. I only had a few CDs with me there, and since it was raining and freezing cold out I spent a lot of time inside, painting and listening to music. *Crash* was one of the CDs I had, and I think that, in a way, it saved my life. I was lonely and depressed, with nothing to do, and I'd fallen into a seriously gray existence. *Crash* woke me up, made me think, and got me through that isolated winter. I got back to California in March of 1998 and bought all the DMB CDs I could find. I continue to be amazed at the beauty, the layers, and the texture of their music. I've seen them live twice now, and I am not ashamed to admit that I am awed by Carter, grooved by Stefan, spellbound by Boyd, moved by Leroi, and completely smitten with Dave. My thanks to the band for making their incredible, beautiful, passionate music. Please don't ever stop, guys.

—*Maria Gaston*

A FAN'S MOM Says Thanks

The following story concerns my daughter, Emily Sentz, and a summer night in 1998 at the Nissan Pavilion in Virginia. Imagine that you are a fifteen-year-old girl and that you have older, twin, college-age brothers who you idolize and who had a band of their own in high school. Your house was then a haven for friends, and music permeated every space. The songs of the Dave Matthews Band have become so imprinted on your brain that you are instantly transported to a specific place and time at the sound of the first few notes. You dream of a time when you can be a part of that scene—not just the little sister who watches and wishes she was older. Imagine one of your older brothers invites you and your friends to go with him and his friends to a Dave Matthews concert. It doesn't matter that the only seats available are on the lawn. You spend hours preparing for the big night. As you sit on your blanket on the lawn your eyes can barely absorb the plethora of happenings around you. Just when you think you are the most blessed girl in the world your brother is approached by a stranger who asks if you all would like seats a little closer to the stage. This must be a joke, right? Other than winning a box of crayons (albeit the coveted box of sixty-four) in a cvs coloring contest at age nine, you've never won anything before. The stranger turns out to be from Dave Matthews's entourage, and you're now sitting in the second row. Afterwards you swear that Dave looked right at you and winked. Maybe he did. This evening will return to memory often over the years, becoming a cornerstone in that fabulous edifice we erect throughout our youth. Dave Matthews, you have the honor of being in my daughter's heart forever. Thank you for your kindness.

—Ann Sentz

COPS HELP OUT DMB FANS

This story deals with getting tickets. One day, me and my friend Kara decided to go sleep out for tickets for DMB's 1998 Hartford shows. We went at, like, three in the afternoon. Of course, since this was a know-nothing town, we figured we'd be first in line. But when we got to the ticket place there was already a small line. We were stunned! So we waited there in line until two in the morning. More people kept showing up and trying to cut in line. Kara and I were very upset. We decided we needed to go somewhere else. Then we remembered another ticket location in the middle of a ghetto. We checked it out: no one was there! We got into my car and gunned it to the location. We were doing almost one hundred miles an hour when a police officer pulled us over. He asked why were going so fast, and we told him we trying to get to another spot for Dave Matthews Band tickets so we could be first in line. The cop laughed and said that if we got him a ticket he'd let us go. Of course we agreed to do it. When the tickets went on sale we got second row. It was great. The cop also got really good seats—so we pretty much broke the law for DMB and got away with it. And the funniest part about all of this is that when we saw the cop tailgating before the concert he handed me a beer.

—Pete Asher

SECRET AGENT
Dave Matthews

This is a short but sweet story. It's about the first and only time I ever met Dave Matthews. One warm June night I was walking around at the Deer Creek Music Center in Indiana. I was waiting for the Dave Matthews concert to start. I had lawn seats, which means you pull up a patch of grass and sit down. Well, I was looking down at the ground and I accidentally ran into Dave Matthews, who was undercover as a Deer Creek worker. I looked up to say excuse me, but nothing would come out. He must have had the same feeling because we both just stared at each other for a minute. His eyes were filled with horror—I imagine he was afraid I would scream his name, but all I could say was, "What are you doing?" He didn't have time to answer me because he was running to the backstage entrance. As I stood watching him he returned his borrowed Deer Creek shirt to its owner and pointed up the hill at me, shaking his head and laughing. I waved back at him. Then the concert started. Thanks, Dave, for that great concert and that wonderfully funny memory.

—Susan Davis

A HUG AND
a Kiss from Dave

No. I wasn't dreaming. The tour schedule said my town. Dave and Tim's tour was coming to my town. I couldn't believe it. I called my friend and we called the ticket outlets and radio stations to no avail. They'd heard nothing. Weeks went by and finally they announced the show. Our souls sang with joy—until we found out that the tickets were only on sale to students of the University of Missouri. We were devastated. It was a really small venue, and it sold out immediately. We were ticketless. As the day grew closer, we tried not to think about our bad luck. There were no extra tickets anywhere. And then—like, a week before the show—one of our local radio stations announced a big fundraiser they were having at a bowling alley for Big Brothers/Big Sisters. Up for auction were two tickets to the Dave and Tim show! Needless to say, we were there early. The bidding went slow, with only two bidders: us and them. But we won! We were actually going to see Dave Matthews acoustic! I cannot describe my happiness to you. There are no words. We soon discovered that our tickets were on the floor, about midway, right next to a taper. (He ended up giving us a tape of the show a few weeks later.)

After an awesome show we headed out into the cold February night, got into the truck, and drove away. We noticed a few people milling around the tour buses and wondered if Dave had come out yet. Just as suddenly as the thought came, we parked and went over by the buses as well. Almost two hours later Dave emerged from the hall. He signed some stuff for folks down by the door, then he walked up the stairs towards us. There weren't too many of us, and I was up against the low rail preparing to maybe get his autograph. He was so calm and so ready to sign our tickets. He was so beautiful up close.

As he signed our tickets, I began to shake because of his closeness. I remember covering my mouth to hide my awe. He signed some other tickets and came back around by me and looked right at me covering my mouth and shaking. Dave smiled a smile just for me, dimples and all. I was so overwhelmed. I found myself saying to him, "May I give you a hug?" He actually walked over to me and wrapped his arms around me, and we hugged a big bear hug. My face was near his so I pecked him on the cheek and the next thing I knew I heard everyone saying, "Oh my God, he kissed her!" We drew apart and I turned away and went and sat down on the sidewalk and started crying. He actually kissed me on the cheek! I laugh now because I'm a lot older than his average fan, and I felt like I was thirteen. The next day my friend presented me with a photo she got with me and him in it. Thank you, Dave, for giving me that moment to cherish.

—*Alisa Hoyt*

WHAT MORE COULD
a Girl Ask For?

The date was July 18, 1999. The city was Denver, Colorado. My boyfriend, Matt, and I were on vacation for a few days, just bumming around Denver and going to see the Dave Matthews Band concert at Mile High Stadium. We had just arrived the night before from Wisconsin, and we decided that since it was nice outside we would go shopping at the 16th Street Mall. Well, actually, I thought it would be a fun thing to do, so of course Matt had to go along with me, being so

DMB CREW MEMBER

Dave, Erin, and Matt, 1999

whipped and all! I was on crutches at the time because of a soccer injury, so we slowly made it around the mile-long street of shops. Then, at about three in the afternoon, it happened. All of a sudden Matt yells out, "Oh my God! It's Dave Matthews!" I thought that he was just playing some sort of sick joke on me, but it turns out he wasn't. There he was, Dave Matthews, sitting outside at the Corner Bakery with some crew members, having some cappuccino. Matt didn't waste another minute and bolted over to meet Dave, totally forgetting me on my crutches. Well, I made it over there eventually, and immediately Dave stuck his hand out and introduced himself (like I didn't know who he was!). Anyway, the first thing Dave did was ask me what the heck happened to my leg. I told him, and he made a few jokes about it. After a few minutes of shooting the breeze with Dave, Matt asked if we could get a picture with him, and of course he said yes. One of the crew members offered to take the picture, so Dave stood up and put his arm around me, and Matt did the same on the other side of me. What more could a girl ask for? Dave Matthews on one side and her boyfriend on the other. The picture was taken and then we said goodbye to each other. As we walked away, I was in pure shock. I could not believe that I had just met Dave Matthews — even more, I could not believe that I didn't scream or make a fool of myself. And now the picture of Dave, me, and my very sweet boyfriend is framed, and it's a reminder of one of the coolest things that has ever happened to me.

—*Erin Tietje*

BONDING
with Boyd

It's difficult to share only one story. My first DMB concert was on New Year's Eve 1996 at the Hampton Coliseum in Virginia. It was packed, and I was so excited. It being my first concert, I had to bring my best friend, Gigi, and two of my brothers, John and Steven. There wasn't assigned seating so we somehow made (pushed) our way to the front of the stage. I couldn't believe how close we had gotten. It was like people just let us through. But when the band came out, some guys started shoving everyone around, even girls, like we were animals. Dave saw this and said, "If some of you guys want to push people around, there are some pretty hefty security guards up here who can help you out." It was hilarious. We were this close through the entire first half of the concert. I was so pumped: Dave's jammin', Carter's bangin', Stefan and Leroi are just sitting back chillin'. I was on Steven's shoulders when it came time for Boyd's solo in "Ants Marching." At this point, I was inches from the stage and more excited than I could ever remember. When Boyd started, I acted like I was playing the violin also. I nearly had a heart attack when Boyd walked to the front of the stage—*right in front of me*—and even though I had no idea what I was doing, everyone started cheering, and Boyd was getting a kick out of it. He and I were so into it. It was like we were the only two there because we were just looking right at each other for the entire solo. I glanced up at Dave, and he had a huge smile on his face, and the other members of the band were laughing. We looked like we were just jammin'. When Boyd's solo was over he pointed his bow at me and everyone screamed. It gives me chills when I think about it. You should have seen it. Thank you, DMB, for giving me your music to rely on during the days "my head won't leave my head alone."

—*Cindy Cline*

"LOOK AT THIS PSYCHO
Dancing His Ass Off" The Dave Matthews

Band is the greatest band ever! My greatest Dave Matthews Band experience was at the July 28, 1999 concert at Lakewood Amphitheater in
Atlanta, Georgia. I arrived at the concert in time to see the end of the
opening act. Dave and Boyd were both onstage playing at the time. Wow!
Well, Dave and Boyd left the stage, and my friend and I went to our seats.
The band opened with "#41" (one of my favorite songs). While I was
dancing and singing, I noticed that one of the security guards had moved,
so I snuck past him to get a better seat. Then, out of nowhere, some guy
came up to me and escorted me to the front row. Then he told me who he
was: one of the guys from Ozomatti, the opening band. He was so nice.
Well, later on in the concert I was up front singing and dancing like a
maniac, and Dave looked down at me and gave me the peace sign. Later
on in the concert, while Dave was mumbling into the microphone, he
pointed at me and said, "Look at this psycho up here dancing his ass off."
It was so cool. Dave is definitely the greatest!

—*Richard Gericke*

WEAR THE HAT! My first, and only, DMB show

was on July 11, 1998 at the Skyreach Center in Edmonton, Alberta. Now,
the band wasn't too popular up here in the cold white North, so they only
sold about three hundred seats, I believe, which made for a pretty intimate
show. Adam, Dana, and I had eighth-row tickets, which was good, because
the whole floor basically rushed the stage. Most of the floor was packed in
pretty tight, dancing and singing. I can't remember what song it was, but
the boyfriend of a girl I know from school tossed his hat up to Dave. It sat
there for the rest of the song, and then we all took up a "Wear the hat!"
chant. So, after our prodding, he picked up the hat and said something
like, "I hope you don't have any funny shit crawling around on your head."
And he put it on to massive cheers. I don't think the guy ever got his hat
back, but I doubt he cared.

—*Jamie Morrison*

BEHIND THE SCENES AT THE "Stay (Wasting Time)" Video Shoot

One of my favorite memories of the Dave Matthews Band was seeing them film a music video. It was in June of 1998, in between the first USA leg and the European leg of the *Before These Crowded Streets* tour. They came back to Richmond to film the video for "Stay (Wasting Time)" in a historic neighborhood named Church Hill. I went down after school to see what was going on. The part I saw them film was the section where the band was playing on a float and wearing white suits. I saw all the band members walk out of their trailer and down the street to where they were to stand. They conversed with people they met as they walked and posed for pictures. Carter was talking to his daughter, who was a flower in the video. The whole street was made to look like a Jamaican town, with brightly colored houses and many people dancing. It was a vibrant atmosphere, which complemented the song well. All the band members had instruments, and they pretended to play along with the song, which was blaring on speakers located along the street. It was a very interesting experience to see my favorite band make a video in my hometown and then see the finished product on TV weeks later.

—Brian Wohlert

A LEISURELY STROLL WITH DAVE

I met Dave Matthews on two occasions. Both times were in NYC at K-Rock (92.3); the first was the most rewarding experience, though. The episode began as a fun-filled DMB weekend. On June 5, 1998 my roommates and I attended a Friday night show at Foxboro Stadium in Massachusetts. Being that we lived in NYC it was a long, three-hour ride, but it was well worth it. Right after the concert we crashed at a hotel. We had a wake-up call at six the next morning so that we could drive straight back to NYC, to the radio station, where we'd attempt to meet Dave.

Our dreams came true when Dave turned the corner carrying his guitar case, accompanied by a few friends. Before entering the building Dave signed a few autographs for us and said that he would be happy to speak to us after he was done with the interview. When Dave was finished he was very willing to sign everything that we had, take all the pictures we wanted, and answer any questions that we had. This made the experience even

ALLISON BALCAN

Dana and Dave, 1998

more magnificent. There were only a total of five people there — my two roommates, two other girls, and me — which also made the experience very personal. After about twenty-five minutes Dave was ready to leave, and he said his goodbyes. He began to walk up 56 th Street, where my car was parked, so we told him that we were not following him but that we were just going to our car. He wait-

ed for us to catch up, and he walked with us. During the ten-block walk Dave asked if anyone had any funny jokes or stories to tell. We informed him that we were at the concert the previous night and that we thought he was fabulous. He asked our opinions on the songs that he played, and I suggested that he should play "The Best of What's Around" more often. We also told him that we would be attending the Giants Stadium concert the next day (June 7, 1998), the finishing part of our weekend-long DMB event. We all said our goodbyes again, and we told Dave how ecstatic we were to meet him and how it was such a great experience. We went home, and we were in awe until ... Sunday's show. Dave and the band came onto the stage and without saying a word went right into the first song — "The Best of What's Around." Dave made my dreams come true the whole entire weekend.

—*Dana Robustelli*

LOSING YOUR FRIENDS AT A CONCERT
Can be a Good Thing

Having traveled with my two roommates to San Jose, California, for the October 29, 1998 DMB show, I must say that the actual show itself was nothing compared to what happened after the show. We lost one of my friends during the show, so we circled the arena afterwards looking for him. After spending an hour doing this, we decided to drive around once more. Instead of finding our friend, we found Dave! He was standing around with a group of about five to eight people, shooting the shit. We screeched to a halt and ran up to join in the fun. He signed two T-shirts and a hat and hung out with us for what seemed like forever (ten minutes). We drank a beer with him, and he promised us a great show next time he came to Colorado. Having brought my guitar with me on the trip, I rushed back to the hotel, which was close to the arena. On the way, I passed our lost roommate, who cursed at me for ditching him! Not believing that we had met Dave, he reluctantly came back to the arena with me. Upon our return, we discovered that Dave had returned to his bus, which looked like it was leaving soon. As the bus started to pull past us, I started jumping and waving my guitar like a madman. Suddenly, Dave appeared out of a window with a smile on his face. He signed my guitar, asked me if I played, and then played a quick riff on it. He then popped back into the bus, and it took off. Imagine that: Dave Matthews played and signed my guitar! I was dumbfounded, and I slept with it that night. I have never—and I never will—forget this, and I am so grateful that Dave took the time to make this fan feel like his only fan. Cheers, Dave!

—*Jamie Santistevan*

UP CLOSE AND
PERSONAL with Dave

One of the most memorable days of my life was March 8, 1999. I was lucky enough to win one of a hundred tickets to a private show with Dave Matthews hosted by a Los Angeles radio station. Two charter buses shuttled us all to a small bar in Hollywood. We walked in to find about ninety seats and a small stage with a stool and an acoustic guitar. Being one of the last ten people inside, I was left without a seat. The ten of us were told to stand at the side of the room, along the bar. We had a poor view of the small stage, so I asked an employee of the bar if we could sit on the ground in front of the stage since there was room in front of Dave Matthews's seat. My request was denied. Shortly after, a radio-station disc jockey introduced Dave, who strapped on his guitar and thanked the audience for coming out to join him. This was the first time I had ever been able to see a show by Dave Matthews or the Dave Matthews Band. For almost four years I had waited for this moment—to see my musical hero perform in person.

I stood in anticipation of the first song he would play, but instead of playing right away Dave looked over and saw the ten of us standing by the bar without seats. He asked why we weren't sitting down, and someone replied that there were no more seats. "Well, there will be no standing during this show," Dave said. He then invited us to sit in the open space on the stage, right in front of him. I could not believe what I heard. From what I had read, people tended to think of Dave as a very nice person, especially compared to other people in the musical field. However, not in my wildest imagination did I think he would allow his fans to sit onstage while he played.

I stepped onto the stage and sat about eight feet in front of Dave. I thanked him for letting us sit on his stage. He smiled and nodded his head in response. Soon after, he played the opening chords to "Too Much." I cannot fully express the feeling I had at that moment. It was a rush of aural joy that I'd never before experienced. The sound Dave Matthews was able to make with only his acoustic guitar and his voice filled the room and captivated his audience. He was only able to play eight songs in the fifty minutes he was onstage, since he had to go appear on the television program *Politically Incorrect*. However, those fifty minutes were simply outstanding. Dave was able to bring tears to people's eyes with his beautiful rendition of "Don't Drink the Water," and he had the crowd clapping and joyfully singing along to "Ants Marching."

As I left the small bar, I realized how lucky I was to have just experienced a very intimate show with one of the best entertainers of our time. Since then, I have been to see two Dave Matthews Band shows — both in the summer of 1999. Though I was not able to sit on the same stage as the band, the memories I hold from those two concerts are just as precious as those from the Dave Matthews solo show. We are extremely lucky to have a band that makes such wonderful and unique music. I hope everyone who hears their music and attends their concerts appreciates the gift the Dave Matthews Band gives to us.

—Patrick Acton

A SPECIAL REQUEST
FOR "Lover Lay Down" I remember a time

when a crazy fan threw a paper airplane onstage at a show. Dave opened it and read it out loud. The note said, "Dave — Please, please, please, please, please, please, please, please, please, please, please, please, please, play 'Lover Lay Down,' because if you do, I'll get laid by my girlfriend, Jill." Dave looked at the guy, then at the note, then at the guy, then at the note, and, after about a minute, he apologized sincerely and said, "I'm sorry, man, but I wrote this song, so if anyone has sex with your girlfriend it's gonna have to be me."

—Jonathan Guez

TOO MANY DAVES

About three or four years ago, when Dave Matthews was on tour with Tim Reynolds, performing an acoustic set, they put on a show one wintry evening at the Indiana University Auditorium in Bloomington, Indiana. At that time, my stepbrother, Dave Thoma, was working as an Indiana University police officer, and he was stationed backstage at the concert. When he passed by Dave and Tim's room, they saw he was an officer and invited him in. Dave told my stepbrother that he needed to come in for a while and relax, take a break. Somebody's pager went off, and everyone started looking around the room, filled with about twenty people, to see who had the beeping pager. It turns out that it was my stepbrother. When he explained that he needed to leave and make a call, Dave invited him to use their phone. Then, better yet, he told my stepbrother (also named Dave) that he'd return the page for him — after all, someone did page "Dave," right? He called, and a girl answered. With a grin, he says, "Hey, this is Dave. Did you page me?" "Is this Dave Thoma?" she asked. "This is Dave. You paged me, didn't you?" The conversation went on like this for about two minutes, until the girl got tired of getting the runaround. "Whatever," she finally replied in frustration. "If you're not going to let me talk to Dave then I'm hanging up!" Click. Little did she know that she was talking to someone better than my stepbrother that night: she was talking to Dave Matthews himself!

—Jeff Smith

DMB FanFare Tip #6:
PRETEND YOU'RE
Someone Famous

November 17, 1998. Toronto, Canada. I'd just seen Dave and the fellows rip it up for the last time ever at Maple Leaf Gardens. What an awesome "#41"! So the show was over, and what was there to do? Go to the Golden Griddle for pancakes? Or go behind the Maple Leaf Gardens and see if the tour buses are there? Now, let me let you in on little info. My friend Aicardo had decided to go to the Dave show dressed up as Maxwell (the singer) — big afro and all. He had on this pimpin' suit with a sweet fur coat. People really thought he was Maxwell; it was quite funny. So we headed behind the Gardens and saw the buses. We got closer and saw Boyd in the window of the bus signing autographs. It's on, baby! We headed over, making our way through the crowd. "Boyd! Hey Boyd!" I yelled. "I want you to meet Maxwell!" I gave Boyd a handshake and I said, "Boyd, I'd like you to meet Maxwell." He looked up, laughed, and gave "Maxwell" a handshake. After a few words and a picture, Boyd signed our ticket stubs and we took off. It was the first time I met a member of the Dave Matthews Band but not the last.

September 11, 1999. Continental Airlines Arena, New Jersey. I'd bought four tickets from the broker two weeks before for, I think, $115 per. Behind the stage! We were the last row in the first section behind Leroi. Upon sitting in our seats we discovered we were in the "turkey-basting" section. The lights were right behind us, and they were blasting us with heat. Adjustments were made. Great show! There were some awesome jams. The concert almost ended in horror, though: it looked like "Don't Drink the Water" would be the last song. Luckily, DMB blew it out with a four-song encore. So then we headed out to the car, ate some food, smoked some greens, listened to some more Dave. "Hey, I just saw Carter over by the bus!" my boy Brian tells me. We head over by the buses and wait ... and wait. Here comes Boyd on a golf cart! I'm feeling the excitement. Damn! He drives right by me. Boyd gets off and quickly signs some autographs, and then he jumps onto the bus. I did get a good picture of him, though. Now, who's next? Golf carts are coming up ... more waiting. Oh my God! It's Dave! Please stop by me. I'm praying. The golf cart stops. Right next to me. Holy shit! Dave gets out, and I'm the first one to greet him: "What's up, Dave! You the man!" I shake his hand and ask him if I can take a picture with him. He replies sarcastically, "If you can make it quick." My pal Ike Luva takes the picture. Dave shakes hands and signs autographs for the fans. So—I met Dave, got a picture of it, the show turned out to be the next live CD, they released the video, and I was in the video (behind Leroi a few times). What a great night! I knew I'd meet Dave one day. Can't wait to meet him again.

—*Todd Pace*

WILL WORK FOR BACKSTAGE ACCESS

This is true. I swear to God. I spent the early months of 1998 eagerly waiting for DMB's new album to be released. Nightly, my friend Matt and I would download DMB songs from the Internet in order to quench our thirst for new sounds. We tried to predict what would be on the album as we listened to samples from the vast Internet collection. At some point that winter I came upon the news that DMB would be playing in Roanoke, Virginia, on April 18th, as a tour opener. As we were at the University of Richmond, our trip plans were made definite on the day the concert date was announced. The months ahead were long and cold, but we pressed on through our classes, waiting for that weekend. When it finally arrived we packed up Matt's Jeep and headed west towards the Blue Ridge Mountains and Roanoke.

Our plan was to camp out on the Friday night before the show, which was to be held Saturday. The drive took us through the freshly green rolling hills of western Virginia and into Roanoke at about 4:30 on Friday afternoon. I thought it would be good to scope out the stadium for the next day's concert since it was to be a general-admission show; that is, first come first served. I wanted to know where we should aim to sit. When we arrived at Victory Stadium I realized that this was, in fact, the first show of the tour. Did that mean they would be doing a sound check on that day before the show? I asked a security guard if there was a sound check planned, and he confirmed that the band was about to arrive. This was becoming all too surreal all too quickly. We decided to wait a bit and see what would happen. Soon after, I saw the purple-and-silver tour buses rolling into the stadium right behind us. Leroi Moore was in the seat next to the driver, and he gave us a wave as they entered. It was at this point that I realized we had to get into that stadium.

Matt and I ended up begging a company that was setting up a pizza tent for the following day to let us work for them for free in exchange for entrance into the stadium. They obliged and quickly assigned us the task of moving large tables around behind the walls of seats. I was bursting with thoughts about the possibilities of the night ahead. We moved one table near the backstage tent. Acting as slyly as we could, we pretended that the table needed to be put backstage, so we walked right through security towards the tent. As we strolled by, there was Dave, mid-dinner, five feet away. I was so stunned that I didn't even realize that Boyd Tinsley was right behind me, grabbing a banana from the food cart. I stopped him when I saw him and tried to articulate the thoughts that I had had since becoming a fan of the band. He was incredibly nice and even took a Ticketmaster envelope into the tent to have the band sign it. He returned to give us the envelope and wish us well, and he even remembered our names. At this point I was sure that I was dreaming. But it gets better. We finished our job with the pizza business and proceeded to hide out in the rows of seats in the stadium.

As the sun began to set, all five members of the band came out onto the stage. Still skeptical of whether or not this was really about to happen, I was assured that this dream was about to take on life when I heard a few notes strummed by Dave over the loudspeakers. Matt and I were the only two people in this entire stadium, and Dave and the band were beginning to play "Jimi Thing." We figured we would be lucky if they played a song or two — but no! Not only did they play a full two-hour-plus set, complete with the new, unreleased album's material, but they also did it with a full light show. I cannot tell you how many times Matt and I simply looked at each other and giggled, realizing what we were witnessing. I believe that a few fans had gathered a few hundred yards behind and outside the stadium to listen, but we were *inside* the empty stadium watching a full show. I would love to put into words the emotion that I felt that night, but no words could justify the experience. Completely blown away by the experience, Matt and I went to sleep knowing that we still had the real show to see the following day.

We arose at six in the morning in order to snatch a spot in the front of the line to get in. Although the gates didn't open until noon, we spent the hours telling fellow fans about the improbable circumstances of the previous night. Disbelief, shock, and amazement were the predictable reactions. When noon finally rolled around, Matt and I were the second and third entrants through one of the gates. We sprinted into the stadium that, only the night before, had been solely ours. We were able to secure two spots against the front railing to watch the show, which would not begin for another four hours. Time, though, did not matter. I was still in ecstasy from our private show. Finally Dave took the stage, and he began, as he had the night before, with the opening notes of "Jimi Thing." I was transported back to the surrealism of Friday night. I swear that during the show I made eye contact with Dave as he sang. He seemed so happy as he looked out at the masses of people who had converged on this small rural community.

The concert was, as expected, incredible. To be able to be that close to something that I love so much was simply the most enjoyable experience of my life. Boyd ripped on his violin and Carter on his drums; Stefan and Leroi added more sweetness to the mix. I sang as Dave sang. I danced as Dave danced. On the drive home to Richmond, Matt and I rerouted the trip to Charlottesville, where we would have dinner at Miller's. As we sat in the dimly lit atmosphere we marveled at the notion that here, at Miller's, was where it all began for DMB. It was a wonderful ending to a dreamlike experience. It's all true. I swear to God.

— *Kyle Smith*

NEVER GIVE UP! The Dave Matthews Band has

been a predominant interest in my life since 1995. I attend their shows whenever they are anywhere in my home state of Michigan, and I know all their songs by heart. My objective was to meet the band—especially Dave Matthews himself. I'm an average person with no connections; therefore, meeting DMB would be difficult. They were in town, and I knew that all the big bands stay at this hotel not far from my house, so I was hoping DMB would stay there, too. I checked it out and, to my relief, they were all there. I met Stefan, and I glimpsed Carter and Leroi, but there was no sign of Boyd or Dave. Luckily, I ran into a really cool member of DMB's staff. He informed me that Dave was eating dinner and when he was finished he would see if it was cool for Dave to come and talk to me. I was ecstatic: I might be able to meet my idol! Unfortunately, I was kicked out of the hotel along with ten other fans because we didn't have rooms. Waiting outside for an hour was no chore because, lo and behold, I finally saw Dave walking in front of the main entrance towards the elevators. Entering the hotel again, I invited him to talk with us, and he graciously accepted, but this guy in his forties pushed me aside. Dave signed the guy's guitar and retired to his room. I was so disappointed. My idol wasn't two feet in front of me and I didn't even get to shake his hand. But I wasn't ready to give up just yet. If Dave spent the extra day between shows in town I would still have a chance to meet this incredibly creative and talented man.

86

Walking on the street the following day, I noticed this guy in a bright red-and-orange plaid shirt. To my surprise that man was Dave Matthews! I approached him and said hello, and when he was finished talking to this other fan he turned towards me. He was so polite and easygoing; he seemed genuinely interested in what I had to say. He was extremely nice and granted all my requests: he autographed a CD cover, posed for a picture, and played "Warehouse" at his next two shows! I was so happy when I heard the song because it made me feel like he remembered my request. It has got to be tiresome having fans approaching you every time you are out in public, but privacy is hard to come by when you fascinate a great portion of the world. The Dave Matthews Band is an icon in the music industry because they represent the better part of music. Acquiring fans the old-fashioned way, by earning their devotion, is not an easy thing to do. Creating such original music that is not formulaic and touches every human emotion makes them unique. I admire how DMB plays music from the heart that, in turn, touches so many other hearts. If you asked me "what would you say" about DMB, I would say that they are, without question, "the best of what's around."

—*Brooke Lotz*

"THAT'S BEAUTIFUL"

The Dave show at Giants Stadium in New Jersey on May 25, 1999, will forever give me the chills. I knew it would be a crazy show. School had just gotten out, I was reunited with my friends from home, and I had not seen DMB since the last summer. Needless to say, I was psyched! My friends and I were hanging out before the show. There were such great vibes spread among the crowd, especially between my friends and I. We were sitting around talking and laughing. It was unbelievable being with them again. As we flowed into the show, Richie, my best friend, and I left our crew and moved to our seats in the second row center. By now, neither of us could contain ourselves. We were bouncing around and jumping for joy. About five minutes later, the lights dimmed and the band graced us with their presence. They flowed out onto the stage. "Is everyone having a pleasant evening?" Dave said. The crowd was going crazy but Richie and I were too thrilled to even open our mouths. We were in awe of the aura that the band brought to the stadium. We were still in amazement when we heard the beginning to "Warehouse." When we heard the intro we looked at one another and grinned — our first show in 1993 had opened with the same song, and it brought back imperial memories. After hearing that song we both knew it would be a night to remember. The night continued to be phenomenal.

The pivotal point of the evening arose during Leroi's sax solo in "Long Black Veil." Leroi was smoothly blowing on the sax; he was in his own little world behind his shades. The stage was glowing a deep magenta hue but Leroi was illuminating. His face lit up as he jammed into his own world, enrapturing the entire crowd, capturing every heart and soul in Giants Stadium. Everyone was enchanted by Leroi's magic; the only movement was the energies flowing through every body. Although the stadium was filled with thousands of strangers, it felt like an intimate gathering of close friends. I honestly could not conceive the night getting any more incredible. But midway through Leroi's solo I glanced at Dave. He was smiling at Leroi, looking so peaceful and serene; he mouthed, "That's beautiful." I smiled and enjoyed the music. At that moment I understood the exact essence of the Dave Matthews Band: understanding and accepting the beauty of everyday life, taking joy in the simple things, being with the people you care about, and — of course — loving the music!

— *Sean Smith*

DAVE'S GOOD DEED

Well, I found out that Dave was filming *Where the Red Fern Grows* in Tahlequah, Oklahoma, and I am in Norman at the University of Oklahoma. I told my friend Jane about it, and we decided to go up there and try to meet him. We drove around for about three hours asking people if they knew where the movie was being filmed. Finally, we found someone who knew where Dave was staying, so we went to the hotel and just sat there waiting for him. While we were waiting, Jane wrote him a letter explaining that her sister had cystic fibrosis and had just gotten out of the hospital. Jane asked Dave to call her sister. We didn't get to meet him that night, but Dave called Jane's sister the next morning and talked to her for about twenty minutes. The next day I went back up and got his autograph and a picture with him. The funny thing — Jane lives in Tulsa and just coincidentally ran into him in a mall there (she didn't get to meet him with me). We were just so impressed that Dave was such a nice guy.

—Josh Hughes

INSPIRATION Courtesy of Carter Beauford

I was at my second DMB show in 1996, and I was desperately trying to meet Carter Beauford, the drummer. I had been a huge fan of him and the band since early 1995. Since I didn't have a pass or know "anyone," I didn't have a chance. After mingling with security and some stage guys and even asking Béla Fleck— who I didn't realize was him at the time—I decided to give up and take my seat for the show. After the show I went to the backstage entrance and was yelled at by a guard to leave because I didn't have a pass. So as I turned around to leave I started yelling, "All I want to do is meet the drummer. I've been trying for so long but because I don't have a stupid pass I can't do jackshit!" Then I felt a tap on my shoulder, and I turned around and yelled, "What?!" This guy says, "You're a drummer?" So I reply, "Yes," and he says, "Drumming brother! You want to meet Carter? Well I can't get you in but if you give me your drumhead I'll have him sign it for you." At this point I was ecstatic! He told me to meet him at the front gate in thirty minutes. So I walked to the gate and waited with the biggest smile on my face. The guards were kicking people out, so I sent my friends to the car and waited alone.

I stalled for time by saying I was waiting for my little sister who was in the bathroom. The guards finally managed to clear everyone away but me. Finally the guard said, "I don't think your sister is coming out." He could tell I was lying, so I told him my situation. Luckily he was cool about it and let me wait some more. Forty-five minutes went by and no sign of the guy. After an hour the guard said, "I don't think he's coming." I sat there, closed my eyes, and prayed that he would show. After an hour and twenty minutes I saw him walking towards the gate flashing the drumhead in the air. He approached me and said, "Sorry it took so long—there were a lot of people." He handed me the drumhead and it read, "Never give up on your dreams. Peace, Carter Beauford." I was almost shaking. After the guy let me see the sticks Carter gave him, I asked how he knew Carter. He told me he worked at the hotel the band stayed at. So I said, "Oh, yeah? Which hotel?" — to which he replied, "Nice try." We had a good laugh, I thanked him, and we both went home. The drumhead is currently hanging on my wall in my apartment in Boston; I am a student at Berklee College of Music. Thanks to Carter's words of wisdom, I'm living my dream as we speak. I graduate in May 2000.

— Matt Iorlano

"DEFINITELY WORTH
5 Hours in the Cold"

I got up early on November 20, 1998 and skipped class so I could arrive early at the Rupp Arena in Lexington, Kentucky, hoping to meet the band. I arrived about noon and immediately saw the tour buses parked behind the venue. I parked my car, and me and my friend Joey got our posters, magazines, and cameras —

DAVIS ARTHUR

Tim and Matt, 1998

just in case. We sat down on the sidewalk and soon met another guy named Dave; he was a musician from Tennessee. He had a guitar, and we sat and showed each other how to play certain DMB tunes and just talked in general about our DMB experiences. We had been sitting

for about thirty minutes when the bus door opens up and out comes Tim Reynolds, who was touring with the band for the fall of '98. I said, "Hey, Tim," and he walked over and talked with us for a few minutes. He signed my *Spin* magazine that had Dave on the cover, and he posed for a picture with me. We talked about the show coming up that evening, and he commented about the Buddhist book our new friend Dave was reading. We asked him about his new, black, long-haired look, and he jokingly said, "It's only appropriate since I'm worshiping Satan now." Then he left to get some coffee. Just a few minutes later a van full of about six guys who had driven all the way from Pennsylvania with no tickets to the show pulled up. As soon as they parked the tour-bus door opened up again. This time it was Stefan Lessard. I asked him if he would sign my magazine and if I could get a picture with him. He obliged both requests, and then I took a picture of the guys from Pennsylvania with Stefan. After, they asked him if he wanted to burn a joint with them, but he said, "No, thanks." Then Stefan pulled me and Dave over to the side and asked if we knew any good vegetarian restaurants in town. Dave knew one called Yesterdays. I immediately offered to drive us all there, but Stefan politely declined and walked away. A little bit later, Tim went back onto the bus with Stefan, Stefan's wife Josie, and his son, Elijah, while we played football in the parking lot. We all waited till around 5:30, but we didn't see any other members of the band except for Carter and Leroi walking around the bus. This day was one of the most exciting in my entire life. The guys were really nice and friendly. Definitely worth five hours in the cold.

—*Matt Anderson*

THE RETURN
of "#40" Explained

You know how "#40" has come back into the play rotation after an almost five-year hiatus? It's even going to be on *Listener Supported*! Well, I like to think that this has a tiny bit to do with me and my friends. You see, we are the ones who got DMB to play "#40" for the first time since May 5, 1995. This happened on December 19, 1998 at the United Center in Chicago. Now, some fans might attest to the fact that the boys had played the song a few times prior to that date, but those were just musical teases. We actually heard it for the first time with words. My buddies and I decided that we were going to get "#40" played, come hell or high water. Since we had tenth-row seats for the show, we decided a huge "#40" sign would get our request noticed. However, I have been to dozens of shows where people do that with no luck. And the people behind them can't see, and that sucks. Then a great wave of an idea washed over me. Why not print up tons of small signs and pass them out to other people? We figured that there might be about three hundred people sitting from the tenth row to the first row. So we got three hundred signs printed, and we were off to the show.

Just after the opening band left the stage we passed out the signs. I was a little worried that security might have a problem with it, but the guy I showed it to just laughed and said good luck. After all the signs were gone (people were grabbing them like they were going out of style), everyone held them up high for the entire arena to see. The place went off the hook! It seemed as though every person in the United Center wanted to hear "#40." (Even though, at the time, most people had never heard of the song.) When Dave and the boys finally got onstage Stefan mentioned something to Dave about the signs. From where we were sitting it was hard to tell what was said, though. After three songs with no response from the band, people stopped holding up the signs. But my friends and I were determined to get the song played, so we kept waving our signs.

Right after "#41," Dave walked around the stage and said something to each band member, pointed to me and my friends, and sang the first verse of "#40"! And there it was — the first blurb of "#40" with lyrics in over four years. Most people looked confused as to what Dave was playing, but we knew what it was, and we were ecstatic. Even though it was unreal that they played it, I still didn't know if it had anything to do with our signs. As it turned out I got my answer from the best possible source: Mr. Matthews himself. People in the Chicagoland area will recognize this. Early in the summer of 1999, it was announced on Chicago's Q101 radio station that DMB would be doing an intimate recording session. They would perform live on the air, and winners of a contest would be able to go there and ask the band questions after the show. No, I didn't win (God knows I tried), but I was listening, and someone asked Dave a question about song requests at shows. I cannot remember what the exact question was, but Dave told them about how, last time he was in Chicago, someone really wanted to get a song played and printed up like a million signs with "#40" on them. Well, that answered my question! Thanks, Dave.

PS: We did the same sign thing when DMB came to Alpine Valley last June. From sixteenth row center, along with two hundred other great fans, we got the first full four-verse version of "#40" since May 5, 1995 as a first encore! The band has been playing it ever since. Thanks again, guys.

—*Ryan Krause*

SCREAM LOUDER!

I never got the pleasure of being up close and personal with any of the guys from the Dave Matthews Band, but I had a really cool experience that included them. On October 26, 1999, I went to their concert at Coors Amphitheater in Chula Vista, California, with my brother-in-law and my sister, who, less than six months after we went to that wonderful concert, passed away from leukemia. I never had a better time with her than I did that night. She was a little sick at that time, and since it was outside I thought we were going to have to leave early because she might get too cold. It was October so the weather was freezing, but the natural high she got from listening to the band made her dance the whole time and her body temperature stayed up. The whole night I was smiling nonstop. I couldn't help myself — my sister was so happy and I was in heaven, being that close to Dave. Even after the concert was over we were standing there screaming and clapping and waiting for an encore — which we did get (since the band is so sweet). My sister kept looking at me like, "Scream louder, Charcee." I kept wanting to say, "Damn! My throat hurts!" But, of course, I did (scream louder) to see Dave again (wink). I don't think any other experience in my lifetime will top this one, especially since it is one of the last memories I have of my sister. But I hope I'll gain lots more memories with the Dave Matthews Band, since the band is a memory of my sister in itself.

—*Charcee Starks*

FAN FLIES FROM ISRAEL
to See DMB
I live in Israel, and I am the biggest DMB fan in the Middle East. I flew to Philadelphia especially to see DMB play. I went to the show (on July 25, 1998), and I was the happiest person in the world because I'd never seen them live and had been waiting for this day for three years. Throughout the whole show I was in heaven. After the show my uncle tried to get me backstage, which was impossible. All of a sudden, I saw that my cousin, who is very pretty, was flirting with someone who had a lot of backstage passes around his neck. I went up to the two of them and asked my cousin, "And who is this?" She introduced me to him, and he told us that if we wanted to go backstage we would have to meet him at the back gate where the band's trucks and buses were parked. I thought I was going to die. We went to the gate, and there were about two hundred other fans, and I thought that this guy had just wanted to get rid of us as soon as possible. But all of a sudden he came up and told the six-foot-tall guard to let us in. I couldn't believe that this was happening! In the end, Dave came out and talked to us for like an hour. I had a DMB shirt written in Hebrew, and he got a kick out of it. I gave it to him, and then he gave me a hug and thanked me so much. That was the best night of my life, and I will never forget it. I thank Mitch Rutman, the band's caterer, who let me in (even though he probably did it for my cute cousin!).

— Yehuda Goldman

4 OUT OF 5 BAND MEMBERS AIN'T BAD
My friend Allison and I were determined to meet the band on their two-night stay in Detroit, Michigan. The band was staying at a hotel right by my house, so we decided to casually walk around downtown and try to run into them. As we were walking by the hotel we saw a lot of kids hanging out on the corner, and we vowed that that would not be us. Little did we know we would be making friends with those people and hanging out with them all day in order to get to meet DMB. First we met their security guard, and I proceeded to offer him fifty dollars if he

would introduce us. Of course he said no. So after a lot of patience and waiting on the street corner, we saw Boyd walk out of the hotel. He was really nice and stopped to sign autographs and take pictures with everybody. Then Stefan appeared, and we chatted with him and got a picture with him. Leroi walked up while we were taking photos with Stefan, and he signed some autographs and asked us for directions to the mall. We were pretty pleased with what had happened so far, but we were still wanting to meet Dave. Finally, at five o'clock, we got a little tired, so we decided to go home. On our way to our car, a man in a van pulled up and asked us if we were waiting to meet Dave. We told him that we were, and he told us to come back in an hour, because he was taking the band and the crew to the Detroit Pistons game that night. We went back to my house and made some calls and rushed back to the hotel. We waited and finally Dave came out. Miraculously, my friend and I got pushed up to the front of the crowd and Dave signed my friend's ticket from the night before while I was busy snapping pictures. We got what we wanted and ran away screaming. We couldn't believe what had happened. The only person we didn't get to meet was Carter, but we figured we did pretty well anyway. The pictures that I have from that day went straight into a frame and are hanging on my wall. I try to show them to anybody who will look at them. Most people just think that my friend and I are completely obsessed and need help. But we got what we wanted: we met the greatest band in the world! Our six-and-a-half hour wait paid off.

—*Cristie Capaldi*

I HAVE NO LID UPON
MY HEAD... On August 12, 1995 I traveled (solo) two

hours up the coast to Santa Barbara just to see DMB play. I arrived early, so I killed time at a bar called Blues, where a local DJ was broadcasting his afternoon show and giving away tickets to the show that evening, along with eight backstage passes. So for about four hours I hung out with the DJ. I ended up losing the drawing for one of the backstage passes, but the DJ pulled me aside and told me to meet him by the side of the stage after the show and he would get me in. I was hooked up! One of my dreams would come true — I'd get to meet Dave, who is/was my inspiration as far as creating music goes.

Before I knew it, I was being escorted into an area backstage with the eight people who were lucky enough to win passes. I remember Dave was leaning against a wall drinking a beer. I took the initiative to say hello first before a crowd of people started to congregate around him. I introduced myself and told him that I didn't have a pen on me, but I just wanted to give him a hug. He put down his beer and gave me the kind of hug that is genuine and warm. (I remember thinking to myself that Dave's the type of person who probably never lets go first.) I asked him if he'd received a letter I had sent to Bama Rags a few months before about his song "Warehouse," explaining how moved I get when listening to the version on the *Recently* album. He sort of looked down at his shoes, embarrassed, and said he got "lots of mail." I laughed and told him not to worry about it. I asked a few other questions about the new studio album (which was to be *Crash*), and then, by that time, I'd say about fifteen or twenty people were trying to get his attention. But before I left I had a random business card that I asked him to sign, and he gladly signed it with a lyric that would be on the next album: "Paul — I have no lid upon my head, but if I did, you could look inside and see what's on my mind. DMB."

— Paul Lemire

HANGING OUT WITH THE BAND

My buddy Scotty and I set off for my first and his second Dave and Tim tour following. Our first stop was Charleston, South Carolina. The show was great! My first Dave and Tim show, and I had fourth-row-center seats. Unbelievable! Before the show, we snuck into the venue and heard some of the sound check. It was kind of hard to hear, but we think they played "Wild Horses" and "Tangerine," along with some other tunes. After the show we darted back to the buses and waited *forever* for Dave and Tim to come out. As it turned out they had left right after the show, and the bus was for the crew. Once the crew left, we packed up and left to find a hotel. As we were pulling away I saw the tour bus on the road, and since we didn't have a hotel room, we figured we'd follow them and stay wherever they were going to. We drove till two in the morning — until we got to Columbia, South Carolina, the site of the next show—and we pulled into the hotel with them. Though we didn't see Dave or Tim, we did see Bagby and Fenton and others. We didn't want to fork out the money to stay at Embassy Suites, so we got a cheap motel room nearby.

The next morning we woke up and went to their hotel before lunch. There we saw Dave and the crew eating brunch in the hotel restaurant. Trying not to be rude, we left him alone and hung out at the elevators until he walked our way to go to his room. Then we met, talked, and took pictures with Dave! Also at the hotel we met an awesome couple named Kevin and Jenn who had been following Dave (and knew him). We talked with them for an hour about DMB and stuff. Then they gave us the location of the next hotel that Dave was staying at, and we left for the Columbia show. Another great show! (Front row this time!) We stayed in Columbia again that night at our cheap motel. The next morning we woke up early and headed for Greenville, South Carolina. When we got there we used Kevin and Jenn's directions and met them at the Hyatt in downtown Greenville. We all hung out in the lobby for about three hours; Dave, Tim, and the crew came downstairs periodically and talked to us. Tim even hung out with us for awhile! Some of the guys we were with didn't have tickets for that night's show, so Dave gave them all free tickets. *Super cool!* We then headed for the show at Furman University, which was the best show of the three we saw (the first "Wild Horses"). Furman has such a beautiful campus. After the show we said our goodbyes to everyone and headed home. One of the best weekends of our lives!

—*Brian Phillips*

DMB AS A TOOL FOR RECOVERY

I was sitting alone in my room. My hands were as cold as ice and my toes had lost all feeling. My mind was spinning with thoughts of a way out as I obsessed over the days ahead. I searched around my room. There had to be something to ease my mind. I picked up the *Crash* CD from Dave Matthews, placed it in the machine that seemed to ease my mind more than the touch of being, and slowly let my body sink into my bed. I pulled the covers up over my head in attempt to lock myself into my own world, and then I listened. I listened to the beat, the ups and downs of the music, the sweet violin, the strumming of the guitar. And, ultimately, to Dave Matthews's voice. My body began to relax and my mind was set free for a brief moment.

For awhile my nights consisted of a lonely date with Dave. I was fighting anorexia, a slow suicide attempt. At seventy-eight pounds and five feet seven inches, I had almost reached the point of no return, but with the help of my doctors and my family I slowly gained the strength and courage I needed to fight the deadly disease. One major step in my therapy was finding quiet time for myself; I could use it to think of nothing at all or to contemplate deep thoughts. For me this time was, and still is, spent listening to Dave Matthews. Every song and every beat brings out a different feeling. I can feel the music run through my blood and soul. "Two Step" lets me sing as loud as possible. And "#41" going into "Say Goodbye" causes me to think about past relationships. "Jimi Thing" and "Warehouse" make me smile, dance, and go crazy around my room. And then there is "Dancing Nancies." Twenty-three and so tired of life — that's me. But I realized that it's a shame to throw it all away. For awhile I just listened to these songs and envisioned them live, but finally I went to a Dave Matthews concert in New Jersey in the spring of '99. A friend of a friend was a guard at the concert, and he somehow slipped me through the gates. He said I was free to roam Giants Stadium but that I would probably end up having to settle for a seat that made Dave look like an ant. With the help of knowing some of the people who check your tickets — and not to mention my smile and the fact that I'm female — I was able to get up to the tenth row!

All the feelings that had brewed inside of me from listening to those DMB CDS were now set free. It was like hearing and listening for the first time again. The feeling was indescribable. I have never danced and moved my body in such a way. I seemed to have spun into my own world. I cared not what anybody else thought of me — all I cared about was myself and the music. It was exhilarating and beautiful. For the first time in my life, I was able to set myself free. Even though it was only for a few hours, DMB generated my soul. The following day, the Roots, who had opened for DMB the night before, played at my college for our Spring Jam. A friend managed to meet them, and they exchanged phone numbers. A few days later, Scratch, one of the band members, called to offer tickets for another DMB show. My friend and I went, and, once again, I shared another exhilarating night with Dave Matthews, the stars, and myself.

—*Erin Pallone*

PRETENDING TO BE DAVE...

This goes to show how loyal DMB fans really are. While I was online, going around in chat rooms, I happened upon a DMB fan chat room. I thought it would be funny to pose as Dave, or just someone close to the band, based on my knowledge of useless info about the band. I didn't get very far. People began quizzing me about information that I don't think God himself knows. I downgraded my gimmick to being a roadie, and I finally had to admit I was messing around. I felt like I was being sacrilegious.

—*John Grant*

DMB FanFare Tip #7:
GET WACKY

My friend Ryan Wood and I went on a six-concerts-in-seven-days DMB spree during the summer of '99. We went to a doubleheader at Polaris Amphitheater in Columbus, Ohio; one concert at Riverbend in Cincinnati, Ohio; and a tripleheader at Deer Creek in Indianapolis, Indiana. Now, Ryan and I are the biggest DMB fans in the world, and you probably don't believe me because everyone else writes that too. But it's true. We are the ones who keep their merchandise store in business; we know a lot about the band and each member, down to minute details; we made a video for MTV fanatics; and we have the edge, because Ryan owns a Gibson Chet Atkins natural-finish guitar (identical to Dave's), and although I don't own Carter's kit, I do my best with my own. They have had the greatest influence on how we play.

Anyway, now that you have some background, you can see that we deserved, and were bound and determined, to meet our idols in person. So, to better our chances, we made bright-yellow T-shirts with huge black letters that said "Dave is my dad" and "Carter is my dad," with descriptions of our fantasies on the backs. Our dream came true during the tripleheader at Deer Creek. After the first concert a security guard saw our shirts and approached us. He had some inside information, and he told us the hotel where the band was staying. He gave us rough directions,but we really had no idea where we were going, so we drove around downtown Indiana at eleven o'clock at night looking for the hotel. Around midnight we finally found it with the help of some local police officers. We removed our shirts so the band wouldn't think that we were psychos, because you must understand that we respect them and realize that they are just like other people except for their incredible musical talent. We really just wanted to sit down and chat with them, even though an autograph or a picture would have been nice, too — just for proof!

We went into the hotel and saw Leroi Moore walking casually into the bar. We both had to look twice before we realized who he was. We shook his hand and complimented him on an awesome show. Then we got kicked out by the bellhops. So we had to wait outside with a few other dedicated fans, even though we knew that if somebody deserved to meet them, it was us. Later, Ryan held his shirt up to the window of the bar before the blinds were closed, and Dave saw it and gave Ryan a smile and a thumbs-up. It gave him a good laugh. Boyd Tinsley was the only member to actually come out of the hotel and greet his fans. He gave us his autograph and we chatted for a short time and he went up to bed. Time passed, and soon we were the only ones waiting outside the hotel. We were on the street because the police said if we were going to stand outside we'd have to stand in the street. We saw Dave and Leroi go up to their rooms, so we were kind of bummed, but we never saw Carter or Stefan leave, so we continued to wait.

Finally the clock struck three in the morning, and Carter and Stefan came out of the bar. We rushed inside and greeted them. I showed Carter my shirt and it gave him a good laugh. I asked him some questions in drum lingo, and we also talked to Stefan for a bit. I asked Carter if he would give me a stick after his next performance and he accepted my proposal. We planned on returning the next night. At the next concert, we were eighth row. When Dave came out to introduce the opening band he recognized our shirts and pointed at us and greeted us with a smile. We went crazy! After the concert, we returned to the hotel and I met up with Carter. The fact that he remembered me was impressive. However, he had forgotten his promise, and his bus had already left, so I never got my used drumstick. All is well though, because we plan on meeting the band again and possibly even opening up for them some day. We remembered numerous questions that we had always wanted to ask them, but that was after the fact. I suppose we were tied up in all of the excitement, mixed with awe, from just shaking hands and talking with the musicians who have inspired us and taught us so much about how to truly speak through our instruments. We felt like we knew them even before we met them.

—Justin Benner

FLANNEL GIRL

"Is this real, or am I dreaming?!" is the first thought that came to my mind when I found out on June 14, 1999 that I would be meeting my idol, Mr. Dave Matthews. I live in Glenview, Illinois, and we have a radio station called 101.9 the Mix. In the beginning of June they announced that they would be holding a contest and the prizes were tickets to a private acoustic concert with Dave Matthews in Chicago on June 15th. The contest was called What Would You Say? The rules were quite simple: send in a picture of yourself and tell them what you would say if you were to meet Dave Matthews. Instead of simply mailing my picture, I made a huge poster and delivered it personally to the station. Everyone was told that the winners would be announced on June 14th. I woke up that morning and listened to the morning show. Sure enough, they called the ten winners, and I was the ninth person they called. I couldn't believe that I had won! June 14th was also the night of the first of two DMB concerts in Illinois. So that night I went to the DMB concert. As the concert went on, I couldn't believe that I was going to meet Dave the very next day. The concert was amazing, but I was excited to get home and sleep so that I'd be rested for the big day ahead of me.

Every contest winner was allowed to bring one guest. I brought my brother, Brian, because he is also a huge fan. On Tuesday morning I woke up very early. Brian and I stopped at a store before we made our way into the city to get Dave a present. We decided to get him flannel pants, because we all know that flannels are Dave's trademark. We got the pants and then drove downtown to the private studio. My brother and I waited for the other winners to arrive before going up. While I was waiting, it hit me that I was actually going to see Dave play a private show and have the opportunity to meet him. A little while later we went up to the studio. It was small and decorated with candles. We sat down in our seats and waited some more. Before I knew it, Dave walked into the room. Tears streamed down my face. I was in the same room with my idol. Dave then played a short, yet unforgettable concert. He played "The Stone," "Bartender," and "Don't Drink the Water." Afterwards Dave got up and walked right past me to the wall where we were going to take a group picture. As he walked by my seat I said, "Hey, Dave. I bought you some flannel pants." He looked me right in the eye, smiled, and said, "Ahhh, more flannel. Nice." Then we went to the picture wall. I literally ran and cut people off to get right next to Dave. He put his left hand around my waist. He looked down at me and said, "Hey, there. What's your name?" I looked right back into his brown eyes and said, "Sarah, Dave. It's so great to meet you." We took the picture, and then I ran back to my seat to get the flannel pants. The radio people got really strict and said, "Hey, you're going to have to leave now." I frowned and said, "I am not leaving without giving Dave the flannels I bought for him!" There was hardly anyone else left in the studio. Dave had his back to me. I walked up, tapped him on the back, and said, "So here are the flannel pants." He took them, looked at me, smiled, took my hand, pulled me in, and kissed me on the cheek! Then he said, "Thanks, Flannel Girl, have fun at the concert tonight."

A few months later, I was on the Warehouse DMB fan club Web site. I was looking at pictures of the band from the 1999 summer tour. I clicked on one of the venues and, to my surprise, there was a picture of Dave wearing the flannel pants that Brian and I had given him! I figured Dave would wear them sometime, but never in my wildest dreams did I think he would wear them at a concert.

—*Sarah Wise*

A GREAT EVENING

A friend and I went downtown — in Memphis, Tennessee — to scope out the hotel the band was staying at while they were on tour in '98. We have friends who own a store in the hotel DMB was spending two nights in while they were in town. They were nice enough to let us come down to try to catch a glimpse of Dave, Carter, Boyd, Stefan, and Leroi. It was a great evening. Some of my closest friends and I shared in a great experience: we were able to meet the entire band. I have a picture of it all, and it is true that a picture's worth a thousand words. I can explain every little detail behind each picture I have. The next day, my friend got the picture developed at a one-hour studio and Dave was nice enough to sign my picture of me with him. Thanks, DMB!

— Brandon Frisch

CHEESEHEADS
I met the band after hiding out with my friend at a hotel in Madison, Wisconsin. Standing in the lobby, the first thing that surprised me was that these guys are huge — I mean, like, tall. Anyway, we followed them outside and asked if we could get a

Pat, Boyd, and Ryan, 1998

picture with Dave. Before Dave answered us he asked if we were "cheeseheads." "Of course we are!" He asked us where our cheese hats and cheese clothes were. I just kind of stood there and smiled until he agreed we could take a picture with him. After that, Boyd said we could also get a picture with him. Little did we know that it was time for Boyd to show his strength and squeeze the cheese out of us. My friend and I both ended up getting two classic pictures out of the deal and a day that I will never forget.

— Ryan Olsen

WHO WEARS BLACK LEATHER to a DMB Concert?

The night of October 4, 1996 was freezing cold, although it was hot as hell inside Madison Square Garden. The mood was filled with excitement and anticipation for the main event of the night. It was only my second Dave Matthews Band show. A friend and I were strolling around the outside corridor of the Garden, checking out the merchandise, when a totally unexpected thing happened. As I walked by an elevator I couldn't help but notice a man waiting for the elevator doors to open. The man was tall and wearing all black leather. "Strange," I thought for a moment, but as I continued to ponder it dawned on me that he was none other than Boyd Tinsley.

"Holy shit!" I shouted. My friend tried to calm me down. "It's not him, it's not him, it can't be," repeated my buddy, and we kept walking. I kept looking back at the man, and there was no mistaking the characteristics — the braided hair, the black leather. I mean, c'mon — who wears all black leather to a Dave Matthews concert? So I ran back towards the man because I decided that this was the only opportunity I would ever have in life to talk to him. We walked by him again, casually saying, "What's up?" to him as we passed. Of course, the fool that I am, I then start shouting, "You're fucking amazing man! You're awesome!" like a jackass. Well, Boyd responded politely, in a friendly way, with a simple, "Hey, guys. What's goin' on?" And with these words his elevator arrived and our experience with Boyd was over. Well, it was a moment I'll never forget. I just wish I'd used the damn camera that was in my pocket at the time.

—Brian Jones

DAVE'S BROCCOLI
(Don't Ask)

It was my fourth time seeing DMB. The show was in Sacramento, California, at Arco Arena on October 30, 1998. I will never forget that night. Not only was I excited because it was the day before my birthday, but I also had the best tickets ever — fifth row! We had made signs, we had a glow stick, and we even made friends with the guy next to us, who was recording the show. After the show, my friends and I decided to wait outside by the buses for the remote chance of meeting any of the band members. After about an hour, my friends left to get the car so we could sit in it and stay warm, while I waited — with much excitement. Since this was a DMB show, I made friends while they were gone. The hour drew near to midnight (my birthday), and I was beginning to lose hope. As the drivers fired up the engines of the buses, my excitement began to diminish. But then the small crowd of about fifteen people began to perk up: there was Boyd! He walked out of the building and boarded the bus, giving us a big wave and a smile. To make the night even better out came Carter with a huge smile on his face, wearing an NBC jacket and his white drummer shoes, ready to meet and talk with us. I was so happy — what a birthday! He gave me a hug and asked me how I liked the show. Smiling from ear to ear, I stood in total awe as he proceeded to sign my ticket. He even wrote "Happy Birthday, Missy," with a smiley face. He stood out there with us for over an hour, telling us stories, seeing people whom he had not seen in years; he was even signing arms and legs while getting names of people who were going to the show the next night to try to get them back-stage. This man was no longer just the drummer in my favorite band. He displayed the kindness of a friend. As he boarded the bus, I could not believe what a wonderful moment I had just experienced. To make things even more cool, as the bus drove off, one of the girls in our cold crew ran after it. The bus stopped and someone handed her what I believe was a plate of leftover food. I don't want to sound weird, but she came over to me and offered me a piece of Dave's broccoli. Without hesitation I said, "Of course!" I don't know how cold it was that night, but it was the most memorable, special time that I have ever known.

— *Missy Davidson*

500 SORORITY GIRLS AND DAVE

In the summer of 1997, I was at the National Leadership Conference of my sorority, ZTA, at the Adam's Mark Hotel in Indianapolis, Indiana, when I heard a rumor that DMB was staying at the hotel, too. The rumor spread fast through about five hundred sorority girls, and then there was a sighting. Dave was there—for real! We found out which room was his and staked it out from a room across the hall. We knocked on his door often, and we slipped a note under it begging him to come out. He finally did, at about four o'clock in the morning. We got to meet him, hug him, and take some really good close-up pictures of him. It was the highlight of my summer and definitely a great conversation piece. I have the picture of Dave and me framed.

—Sara Aderson

"DAVE MADE FUN OF MY VOICE!"

My Dave Matthews experience is somewhat different than the usual "I screamed, 'I love you, Dave,' and he gave me a thumbs-up," or the old, "I met Dave and he said my necklace was cool." That stuff is all well and good, and I wish I had a story like that to tell, but I find mine to be more humorous than most. It's Tuesday, February 2, 1999, and the day has finally arrived when I can count the hours rather than the days till I see Dave pick up his guitar and play for the crowd that's beyond lucky to be there. Since I could only get two tickets for this concert, "An Acoustic Evening with Dave Matthews and Tim Reynolds Live at Beacon Theater," my older sister is coming with me. We hop a train into New York City. We arrive at the theater, and I know we have pretty good seats because we started calling Ticketmaster two hours before the tickets went on sale. The usher shows us to our seats. I am overwhelmed with excitement. We are sixth row center! The concert starts. It's amazing—as all Dave concerts are. In the middle of the show, after Dave has just finished a song, everyone screams out what they want to hear next. I think, "Why not join in?" So, in a high-pitched voice I scream, "Play 'Little Thing'!" Over all the other screams he hears my loud mouth, and he mimics me, yelling, "Little Thing, Little Thing" in my high-pitched voice. The crowd laughs, and I freeze. Dave smiles and goes on with the concert. Dave never played "Little Thing," but he did give one of the best concerts I've ever been to. And how many people do you know who can say, "Dave made fun of my voice?"

—*Caitlin Sheehy*

FAN HELPS DAVE
AVOID FALL
It was January 27, 1997, at Connecticut College, in New London, Connecticut. Dave and Tim had just finished the most amazing concert I have ever heard, never mind seen. My friend Kate and I decided to wait outside by the bus in hopes of getting a glimpse of Dave. We finally got outside after filing out of the approximately three-hundred-seat theater, and we were welcomed by freezing rain and snow. We were the first ones to get to the area near the bus, so I wrote my name in the dirt on the side of the all-black tour bus. Then I waited with my legs against the makeshift barricade. More and more fans started gathering around and behind us. Finally, after we'd waited about forty-five minutes in the freezing rain, the back door of the theater opened and Tim came running out. He was running like his life depended on it. He slapped me five as he passed, and then he jumped into the bus. I still can't believe I actually touched his "magical" hands. Soon after, a first-story window opened and a leg appeared, then an arm, then a head. "It's Dave!" someone yelled. Dave had the funniest expression on his face—like, "Holy shit!" Then he ducked back inside.

Finally, after about an hour and a half, the back door opened and Dave came strolling out. I was the first person he saw, and he came right up to me and shook my hand. He was wearing a hemp pullover with the hood up, and his eyes looked a little glassy. "Hey. How ya doing?" he asked. And that's when I felt the pressure of the crowd pushing on me. Then the barricade gave way. The crowd pushed me right into Dave. There was nothing the two campus security guards could do but watch. Dave squeezed my hand, holding on, because the sidewalk was iced over. With me holding Dave up, we made our way to the bus, and I helped him on. He took a couple of steps up then turned around and gave me a look to thank me.

It was absolutely amazing. I just stood there for awhile thinking about what had happened, then I got into my car, which was parked right next to the bus. As we drove away, I looked through the rearview mirror of the car at the glow-in-the-dark alien head in the front window of the band's bus.

— Michael Berger

"OH MY, I WAS SQUEEZING
You a Bit Too Hard,
Wasn't I?" Well, first I must say that being told I was going
to have the chance to meet Dave floored me. As if it wasn't enough to have watched the December 7th Worcester Centrum show from the fifth row, a show that had one hell of a set list and was so full of energy. What a dream to hear "Halloween" live and then meet Dave in person. I can say that other than the birth of my three kids nothing will top this. I was brought into a small room with about forty or fifty other people. We sat around for a few minutes drinking some complimentary sodas. I sat right by the door so that Dave would walk right past me. So, we're just sitting there and in walks David John Matthews, looking somewhat tired and wearing black pants with white stripes on them and a red, long-sleeved T-shirt, with what I believed was a Heineken or a Rolling Rock tucked under his arm (after a careful examination of the photos I see it was actually a Sam Adams). He walked right in and looked at me and then did a double take and looked back at me again. I thought I was dreaming it, but the girls with me said, "Wow, he looked right at you!" He mingled around a bit, graciously signing autographs, and I decided to approach him — after a little prompting. I went up to him and I was so shell-shocked to be standing inches away. My legs were shaking and I just said to him, "I'm pretty nervous, but I wanted to talk with you a minute and ask if you would sign my ticket stub for me." He said, "Oh, sure. I'd be happy to." So he took my stub and signed it and drew a little peace sign on it. He also signed a little piece of paper I had. I said, "Would you mind putting my name on that for me?" And he said, "Of course. What's your name?" So I said, "Carolyn." And just to hear this man repeat my name was like I died and went to heaven. He said, "Is that spelled 'lyn,' Carolyn? So I get it right." In my mind I was thinking, "Spell it anyway you want, sweetheart." He could have signed it to "Bill" — I wouldn't have cared. When he was done, he handed me the stub, and I

said to him, "I want you to know that your music touches me so much and it's so therapeutic for me to listen to." I told him that I had been going through a rough time in my life and that his music had helped me cope. He grabbed my arm from underneath, sort of holding onto my elbow, and squeezed it real tightly and said, "I'm so glad that it touches you that way because it does the same for me." Then I thanked him for taking the time to speak with me and walked away ready to faint.

BOBBY NICKERSON

Dave and Carolyn, 1998

I went back to my seat and was just awestruck. Just to be in the same room with him and watch him interact was the coolest experience for me. I sat with some friends and talked about how much I wished that I had my camera with film. I had used the film up during the show, never thinking I would actually have the opportunity to meet Dave. Luckily, I was able to get my hands on a camera to have a photo taken with him. I waited for a good time and approached him again. I asked if I could just take one more minute of his time, and he said, "Oh, sure, sure." So I said, "I would love it if I could get a photo of us together." I handed the camera to a man standing next to me. He turned out to be a photographer for *GQ* magazine! Wow, did I pick the right guy to ask. Dave put his arm around my waist and he squeezed me so hard that all I could think in my mind was, "Please, God — don't fall on him!" He was holding on to me with such strength I could hardly stand it. My foot was off the floor, he was holding so tightly. The feeling of standing there being held by this guy and having my arm around him as well is just something I cannot put into words. The guy from *GQ* said, "Okay guys, I do this for a living, so show me some *pout*." It was so funny, and Dave started acting goofy, and I just kept looking at the camera smiling so that I wouldn't look away and ruin the shot. I'm not sure what the hell he was doing. When the photos were taken Dave turned to me and said, in his very English/South African accent, "Oh my, I was squeezing you a bit too hard wasn't I?" I looked right at him and said, "Don't worry about it. The pleasure was all mine." Then I thanked him again and walked away with a big grin on my face that I thought would be there for life. I sat down again and just watched him move around the room, responding so genuinely to his fans. He really cares about them and takes the time to talk to them, and I think he realizes just what he means to people. He's so gracious. At one point a man who was relaying messages to him was saying that they wanted to know how long he would be, and Dave responded, saying, "I still have some people to talk to. As soon as I talk to everyone I'll be along." Can you believe that? He is truly a sweet man, and I will never, ever forget meeting him.

—Carolyn Sabbatelli

A STORY Guaranteed to Make You Cry

In 1997, I proposed to my college sweetheart. As I was (and continue to be) a huge fan of the Dave Matthews Band, I thought it would be interesting if I sent a letter to the band asking them to play at my wedding. Though everyone laughed at my idea, I felt that I had to give it a shot. After all, I believe in long shots. Over the Thanksgiving vacation of that same year, my fiancée was involved in a tragic

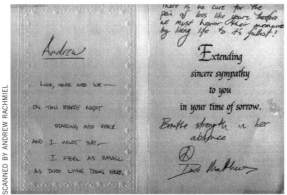

accident and was instantly killed. Through many, many months of heavy grieving and counseling, I found the most comfort in listening to the words of the Dave Matthews Band. I have read many articles on the life experiences that each band member has been through, and I have always been able to relate to their experiences through their music. Prior to the date our wedding was to have taken place, I felt the need to send a follow-up letter to Dave and the band, letting them know that I would have to take back my request. Though I still cannot even summarize what happened that terrible weekend in November 1997, I did give them a very brief explanation. Several weeks after sending the second letter, I received a card in the mail from Dave Matthews himself. This couldn't have come at a better time in my life, as I needed to hear exactly what Dave wrote: "We must honor their memories by living life to the fullest. Breathe strength in her absence." I knew that as I read those words they came right from Dave's heart. It was only recently that I had the opportunity to thank Dave for this unbelievable gesture. I won a local radio-station contest to see a private performance given by Dave Matthews for twenty listeners. After the show, I had only a few seconds to express my gratitude. I shook Dave's hand and said, "I know you don't know me, nor am I allowed the time to explain our connection, but I just need to say thank you." Dave smiled, said, "Cheers," and that was it. For musicians, I can only imagine that the ultimate goal is to learn that their music has deeply touched and inspired the life of a fan. The Dave Matthews Band has done far more than that for me. Dave's consideration and thoughtfulness at a very tough time in my life has been a much-needed inspiration for me to this day.

—*Andrew Rachmiel*

DMB FanFare Tip #8:
GET A DMB LICENSE PLATE

It was a beautiful September morning when the long trek from Virginia to Jersey began. My friends and I were off to see the Dave Matthews Band at the Continental Airlines Arena. The fun began as we approached the arena. Other fans honked and waved to us as they drove by, seeing that we were huge DMB fans, too. I was driving the "Davemobile"—my car license plates say DAVE LVR and the bumper of my car is plastered with every DMB logo out there. We were all psyched. During the show I was jamming to every beat. I even had my DAVE LVR plate with me in the arena, and the night took another step up when I was filmed for PBS with the license plate during "Two Step." The night, the show—it was all perfect, and yet there was more to come. It just so happened that the Davemobile was parked in the back of the arena. As we were leaving, my ever-so-observant friend noticed a huge charter bus with a crowd of people gathered around it. We decided to investigate, and the four of us quickly tried to get the license plate off the car again, just in case. We were just in time to see Carter Beauford getting into the bus.

Then came Boyd Tinsley. I was more than lucky because he walked right over, signed my license plate, took a picture, and then walked onto the bus. I could not believe what was taking place. I never thought a license plate would bring me so much attention. A DMB crew member took the plate from me and walked towards the arena. I was saying a silent prayer, and my mind warped into fantasy mode, and I pictured the man saying,

Kristen's license plate

"Come with me, and we will show Dave Matthews the plate together." But he just brought it back to me. A group of fans stood waiting for nearly ninety minutes until Dave left the arena. As he walked over to the barricaded group of fans, my friend grabbed the license plate from me and jumped over the barricade! She ran to Dave and asked him to sign the plate! He did! My heart was beating so fast. Saying I was excited does not begin to explain how I was feeling! As Dave made his way down the line to say hi to everyone, I told him frantically that he had actually signed *my* plate, and I thanked him again and again during my whole nineteen seconds with him. He looked at me, took my hand, and did a special little handshake. I was absolutely starstruck, despite telling myself I would be one hundred percent normal! We all watched Dave get onto the bus, and the band pulled away for the airport. The car trip home that night was definitely like no other. I had met Dave and Boyd! I can't wait until the next show. If Carter, Leroi, and Stefan could sign my plate, I would frame it. Now it just hangs in my dorm room. What a night! What a night!

— *Kristen Scheerle*

A LITTLE WHITE LIE
Never Hurt Anyone... Well, it all began on

September 11, 1999, when I got a ticket to the *In the Spotlight* special.
I went to the show with a friend I had just met at college, and it was amazing.
After the show, we were determined to meet Dave and the guys. We waited
outside of the Continental Airlines Arena in East Rutherford, New Jersey,
and we were set on camping out. We were going to wait all night just to
shake Dave's hand after an incredible performance. So I waited, with four
of my friends, and finally he came out and quickly shook all of our hands.
He made sure to acknowledge everyone and make eye contact with everyone. But we were determined to have a conversation with him. We were
on a mission. We got into the car and followed the bus. Yeah—we felt
like stalkers, but we were determined. It was such an amazing show and
we just wanted to tell him that and thank him. So, in a caravan of fellow
psychotic fans, we followed the band. Then their large black bus pulled
into Teterboro Airport (a small airport in New Jersey), and the gates closed
behind them. We were so disappointed. About twenty-five people were just
standing there waiting. The guy at the gate warned us that they would call
the cops, so my friends and I decided to clear the parking lot. We started
yelling, "The cops are coming! Everyone leave!" We then pretended to get
into the car, and we watched everyone else leave. Soon we were the only
ones left, so we went to the gate and made conversation with the guy there.
Then we spotted Dave getting off the bus; he was about to board the plane.
I started yelling his name and telling him that we had cleared the parking
lot. He smiled and graciously came over and talked to us. It was amazing.
He signed autographs and we chatted about the first time I had met him.
After such a long night, he still was so polite to us and chatted as his plane
waited. It just proved to me that he is not only a great musician but also a
great guy. I had a letter in my pocket that I had written to him just in case
I ever met him again, and I was so nervous to give it to him. I had taken it
with me to every concert. Nervously, I handed it to him, and he seemed so
thankful. He put it in his pocket and thanked me. Whether or not he read
it makes no difference to me. I am sure that he did, though, because that
is the kind of guy he is. It was amazing to meet the man who has been
able to express so many of my thoughts and feelings in his own words. I
will never forget that night, and I can't wait to meet Dave again!

—*Katie Dean*

AN IDEAL TIME
for a Power Failure February 1996, Colby

College,Maine. Dave and Tim. While most people would consider their wedding day or the day their first child was born their greatest day in life, at twenty-three mine would have to be a brief encounter with the Waterville, Maine, police, which led to my first meeting with Dave Matthews. After traveling four hours through a blizzard in a '67 Mustang my friends and I decided to partake in a little preconcert relaxation therapy. Mine consisted of a little vodka-Snapple contraption while my friends engaged in something a little more obvious to the patrolling campus police. The campus police officer was assured of illegal activities when our driver opened the door and let out the car's entire contents of smoke into her face. A nice young Waterville police officer was called to the scene and, although we had never met before, he spread me and my friends across our Mustang hood and felt us up. He took the remaining evidence, leaving us with a court summons, and we arrived at the concert just in time for the encore. This was my first Dave and Tim concert, and I was a little pissed off, to say the least. We walked around the clean-up scene afterwards, hoping for a Dave sighting and avoiding the four-hour drive back. Then I had to relieve myself of the remains of my vodka-cranberry.

Walking back from the men's room I did a double take to see Dave in a room signing autographs and drawing figures on T-shirts. Honest to God, I prayed just for an opportunity to introduce myself and express my admiration for his music. At that moment, every light in the building except for the room Dave was in went out. Security left the door for a moment and — sorry — I snuck in as fast as I could and as deep into the crowd as I could until I bumped into someone. That someone was Dave. I extended my hand with an awestruck look on my face and said, "Hi, Dave. I'm Eddie." It was simple but good enough for him to pull me aside and chat one-on-one for a few minutes. By far the most down-to-earth and nice person I've ever met. Funny as hell. I got a little inside info on the upcoming album at the time (*Crash*), and I received an autograph. Dave gave a peace sign on his way out and said, "Thanks, ya'll." No, thank *you*, Dave. PS: The court threw out the case due to "lack of evidence." Who said Waterville cops don't know how to have fun?

— Eddie Gaines

A LASTING
IMPRESSION... My fortunate meeting with Dave

Matthews occurred on February 3, 1999, before the Dave and Tim concert at Penn State. I'm currently a student there, and on my way home from class that day, stoked about the concert that evening, I bumped into Dave and his buddy on their way to do some shopping. There wasn't a crowd around them, and Dave wasn't standing out at all. He was dressed in casual slacks and a dark jacket. At first I didn't recognize him, but because I've spent many hours listening to his music, watching his concerts, and seeing him in countless magazines, I soon did — and I couldn't believe my eyes. I quickly approached him and shook his hand and expressed my appreciation for his music. We then got into a conversation a little off base from music. I asked him about his health and how he's feeling — he'd canceled the Monday before due to sickness. He said he was doing better and would do the show that night. I jokingly said, "Well, better lay off the drugs — you'll last a lot longer. I want to see you perform again." He thought that was quite funny and responded sarcastically by saying, "How about I do some crack tonight, then? Think that will help?" We had a laugh and talked about some other topics, which lasted for about twenty-five minutes, and then more people gathered. Afterwards, I was able to get a picture of him and a few signatures.

Later that evening, during the show, after about the fourth song, he mentioned his encounter with me. I thought this was amazing. I was getting recognition from Dave Matthews onstage. He started by recalling how he bumped into me and our conversation about drugs and him being sick. He then said he was thinking at the time, "Is this kid trying to be cool and show off, or is he caring, or is he just a plain idiot?" The crowd laughed because of Dave's actions and voices. Even though all of this was unexpected, the impression I made on Dave that day was priceless — it was an experience that won't be forgotten. Afterwards my friends approached me, and we had a laugh about what Dave had said when I told them what had happened earlier on that day. Little did I know that I would meet Stefan, Boyd, Carter, and Dave again ... but that's another story.

— Peter Huang

CRYING ALWAYS WORKS

"You just *gotta* let us in!"

It was May 29, 1998, in Chicago. Me and my friend Jade were getting ready to go to the DMB concert, and we had a good vibe going on that day. We got to the concert and found front-row parking—we knew it was going to be a good day! And considering that we had already met Dave once before, we knew that we could do it again. We crammed our car into an imaginary spot right by the backstage gates, just in case we had to stalk the buses. Concert time. Good seats—could've been better, but good enough. We drank, laughed, and sang along to the songs we all know and, most of all, love. Before the show we'd spent an hour convincing a security guard to let us backstage because, "We just have to get back there!" So when the encore was over we ran like there was a riot going on behind us, got to the backstage gates, and cried to get in. And he let us in! We were like nine year olds, hiding in the corner so we wouldn't get kicked out, and then Dave came out! We almost *died!* He started signing autographs, joking with people, and he was drinking a Heineken. I wanted to be that bottle! So he came up to us and signed our stuff. I gave him a hug, and he kept looking at us—well, you know, two young cute girls. So after we had to leave we waited outside and followed the buses. It was awesome: we were in between the two buses, taking pictures and screaming. We got all the way to downtown Chicago. We saw Dave get off one of the buses on Michigan Avenue, so we slammed the car into another imaginary spot in the middle of what could be a highway and ran over to him and walked down the street with him. He put his arm around us and just talked to us like we were normal people. Then he got into a cab and left—just like that. But we know he will see us again some day. And that just about concludes our adventure with Dave!

—Jennifer Letrich

DMB FANFARE: THE EPIC STORY

I guess that one could say it all began on the Fourth of July, 1997. This was the day that I met Dave Matthews. The reality is that it was going on long before this date, but for the sake of just having a concrete date, we will go with this one. At about ten in the morning on the Fourth of July, in Newport Beach, California, I was at my friend Rob's house preparing to have a day of fun in the sun. Rob doesn't really care too much for the Dave Matthews Band, so I proceeded to tell him that he'd better learn to appreciate them, because one day Dave was going to be his brother-in-law and Rob wouldn't be invited over for dinner if he couldn't think of anything positive to say. Needless to say, the only way to start a great day in the life of La'Sundra is to listen to a little Dave Matthews Band. My song choices for the happy day were "Watchtower" and "I'll Back You Up." At around 10:30, we left to go and get some food down by the marina. We got to a place by the water, and we sat there for about thirty minutes, but no one ever came to take our order. We got pissed off and decided to just grab some sandwiches at a nearby café. Again we had problems: they put some black-olive crap on my sandwich. Needless to say, I took it back inside to have them make it over.

As I was waiting for my new sandwich I turned around, and who was just standing there? None other than the man himself: Dave Matthews! My brain literally jumped! I instantly thought of my journal. For about a year or so I had been keeping a journal just for him — my thoughts on how the music makes me feel, how the thought of him makes me feel. I carried this journal with me everywhere I went on the off chance that I would meet him. My day had finally come. My voice was a little shaky, but I managed to call his name. He looked up at me as if he were in shock that someone at a little café recognized him. I told him my name and proceeded to tell him about my journal. Then I asked him if he would take the time to read it. He agreed. I watched as he read. It could have been my imagination, but he seemed to laugh and smile in all the right places. When he was done, he smiled and told me that it was very nice. By this point my legs were shaking so badly that I felt like they were going to walk away without the rest of my body. The band was playing the next day at Irvine Meadows, and I just happened to have a camera with me. To make a long story short, I took pictures with Dave and told him that I'd see him tomorrow at the show. He gave me a long hug, and we said our goodbyes. Wow, what luck! It couldn't possibly get any better — but it did.

The next day I got up at eight in the morning to wait for DMB to get to Irvine Meadows. "Why?" you might ask. Well, I was so taken aback when I first saw Dave that I didn't really get to talk to him, so I was determined to see him again. To make a long story short once again, I broke into Irvine Meadows. This, I might add, was a very dirty and difficult task. There were barbed-wire fences, prickers, and even a stream to cross. But where there is a will there is always a way. I hid out in the bathroom for about forty-five minutes, just waiting for some sort of a sign. I got one! Dave began to sing: it was sound-check time. I walked out into the stands trying to look as if I belonged. I sat about fourth row center and watched the band do the sound check. I don't really know if Dave remembered me from the previous day, but he looked at me, smiled, and threw me a nod! (Sigh.) I was still determined to speak to him, so when the sound check was over I went backstage to try and find him. He was nowhere to be found. Aha! But Carter was! I stopped Carter and asked if he would take a picture with me. He agreed. I then began to tell him about breaking into Irvine Meadows, and I asked if he could get me a backstage pass or something. He said, "I'll be right back," and he returned with two orchestra-seat tickets. Wow! I told him thank you and asked if he would pass along a letter that I had written to Dave. "No problem," he said, and then he told me to make sure that I got good money for that extra ticket. I smiled and said goodbye. Wow! Carter Beauford! At this point I decided not to push my luck, so I went back out to the parking lot to sell my three extra tickets. I sold the two loge seats for fifty dollars apiece and the orchestra seat for one hundred dollars. How could it get any better? It did. I realized that I didn't have very much green, so I asked some random guy walking by if he had any extra, and he gave me a handful and walked away! How is that for luck?

I'd always thought that particular weekend would go down in history as the best weekend of my entire life. I listen to the Dave Matthews Band every single day. If you find something that makes you happy, I say go with it, no matter what anyone says. On March 21, 1998, I got the "fire dancer" tattooed on my back. People like to poke fun and say that I'm nuts, but who cares! I made a promise to myself that the next time the band came to town I would take time off work and go to see them. That time came. They were playing a show in San Francisco and another at

Irvine Meadows again. On April 4th I got up at three in the morning. Why so early? Well, I've always believed that the early bird gets the worm. Tickets for the Irvine Meadows show were to go on sale at 10:30 — hey, what's seven and a half hours! Then something happened that made me think my Dave luck had run out. Yes, I was the first in line (the next people didn't show up until around 8:30). But they decided to do wristbands! Fuck! I ended up almost second to last in line. Tears. Needless to say I had the third person in line buy me a ticket, but I still ended up in the loge. The next day tickets went on sale for the show in San Francisco. I was on hold for forty-five minutes trying to get a seat. I ended up on the lawn. But, hey — at least I was going! I drove up by myself — it actually only took six hours! I stayed with my friends Kris and Sarah.

The show was amazing! I couldn't wait to hear the new songs played live, and let me tell you it was everything that I could have hoped for and then some (not to mention the fact that I saw Chelsea Clinton at the show). I returned home on Monday and made my plans to see the boys taping *The Tonight Show* the next day. This was when I had planned to see Dave again. They sang "Don't Drink the Water" with Béla Fleck sitting in on the banjo. I had read that Béla was playing that night at the Coachouse in San Juan Capistrano. The taping of *The Tonight Show* wasn't over until about six o'clock in the evening, and I figured the guys would be catching Béla's show after it. I literally ran to my car to try and make my way to San Juan as quickly as possible. As I was running I saw this purple tour bus fly by. I thought to myself, "Hmmmm." I got on the freeway, I saw the bus again — hmmmm. The traffic was terrible. The bus jumped into the carpool lane and was gone. The traffic finally broke up, and I saw the bus again in between Long Beach and Huntington Beach. I decided to catch it. I passed it and then got around to the bus driver's side. He began waving at me, and who came up to the front of the bus? None other than Carter Beauford! I reached into my bag and pulled out the picture that he and I had taken at Irvine Meadows the previous year. He smiled, so I followed the bus to their hotel — the Huntington Beach Hilton.

There were about six other people waiting for them who wanted guitars signed and whatnot. No one got off the bus. Finally the door opened and this guy got off the bus walked over to tell me that I could go ahead onto the bus if I wanted! I got on the bus, and Carter greeted me with that beautiful Carter smile. I showed him the picture again and asked him if he remembered me. He said yes. I proceeded to meet Leroi, Boyd, and

Stefan. They told me to have a seat. I ended up watching the end of the Bulls game with them in the tour bus. Wow! Carter asked me what my plans were for the evening and told me that I could hang out with them if I want to. Of course, I asked where Dave was, and Carter told me that he had to stay up in Hollywood to do some PR stuff. Needless to say, I stayed. Carter went to take a shower, which left me to hang with Lupé for a little while. Lupé Lupé Lupé! The greatest guy. He was so nice to me, you would not believe it. He gave me the skinny on who to call if I was ever in need of ticket for any of the shows. I didn't get home until around two in the morning. Partying with the Dave Matthews Band!

Lupé told me that they'd give me a call in the morning to give me the plan for the concert day (passes, and so on). I got the call at about eleven. They were checking out at three that afternoon, so they said to come over then. So I did. I pulled up, and Lupé was standing by the bus. So were about ten people waiting to get their guitars signed. Out walked Dave. He stopped to sign the guitars and proceeded to walk over to Lupé and me. I could tell that he was wondering who the hell I was. As he got closer, he told me that I looked familiar. I showed him the picture from last year and asked if he remembered taking that picture. He asked me where it was, so I reminded him, and he said that he did remember. Meanwhile, it was check-out time. Dave told Lupé and me how he wanted to go and grab a latte before they left but he didn't have enough time to walk to the coffee shop. Hmmmm. "Hey, Dave! I've got my car right here. I can take you over there real quick." "Really?" he said. So little ol' me and Dave Matthews rode off in my car to get coffee! There we were engaging in small talk, and I jokingly told him that he could be kidnapped. He smiled and said, "Oh, well!" He leaned over and slowly, gently kissed my shoulder. I melted. Did he have any idea? Wow! E-gads! I forgot to tell you the first thing he said when he got into my car. "What happened to your neck?" Of all the times to burn my neck with a curling iron, I had to do it the week I met Dave again! Anyway, we got back to the hotel, and he leaned over and kissed me on the cheek, saying, "Thank you!" Oh, and while he was in the car I got him to sign my journal. Can you believe I didn't even get his autograph the first time that I met him?

Okay, so then it was time to get over to the venue. I followed the tour buses over, and I got VIP parking! I went backstage, got my pass, and waited. It was sound-check time again. There I was, fourth row center for the second year in a row, watching the Dave Matthews Band play only for me! Carter waved from his drum set and Dave smiled. "Rapunzel" is what they played (the year before they played "Recently"). I felt as if none of this was real, like I was going to wake up from a great dream soon — but I never did. It was *real!* I don't know if it was because I felt that they were now my friends, but I can honestly say that it was the best DMB show that I had ever seen. When it was over, I went backstage to say goodbye to the boys. Dave and Boyd were the only ones to be found. I walked over to Dave, who was among a crowd of people. He stopped signing autographs. I told him that I was leaving and I just wanted to say goodbye and tell him how much I enjoyed the show. Again he said "Thank you for the coffee," and he kissed me on the corner of my mouth. Then he said goodbye. Wow! Sigh ... it was all real. Just when you think that things can't get any better! For the record, I have learned a lot through this experience. Needless to say, I would never again make a profit on selling a ticket to see the Dave Matthews Band play. If they even mean one quarter as much to someone else as me, then that person deserves to see them without having to pay an arm and a leg. Scalpers suck. (But the guy who paid the hundred dollars for my extra ticket sat next to me at the show, and he said it was worth every penny!)

—*La'Sundra McDaniel*

"WHAT THE HELL Are You Doing Here So Early?

On December 29, 1996, me and a bunch of my friends headed to the US Air Arena right outside of Washington, DC. We timed it a little early and got to the arena way before anyone else, including the band. As we sat in the parking lot trying to decide what to do to waste some time, DMB arrived. The last bus to pull in was burgundy in color, and there was Dave — sitting in the front, watching TV. We were ecstatic. He got off his bus and came over to us. "What the hell are you all doing here so early?" he asked. We just looked at each other in disbelief. I think I freaked him out, because I wouldn't let go of his hand when he shook mine. The concert was awesome, and it was a day I will never, ever forget. We all got our ears pierced to remind us of the rare event.

—*Chad Massaro*

WRITE A NOTE

It was a cold night in February 1997, and my friends and I were in West Point, New York. The Dave and Tim concert was about to begin, and my friends and I wrote a note to throw onstage in hopes that Dave would read it. I walked up to the stage and threw it on, but five minutes later a stagehand picked it up and put it in his pocket. We were depressed because we figured Dave would never get the note. Boy, were we wrong! When he and Tim came out, they first introduced Stefan, who would be joining them that night. Dave then said, "Before we start, I just have to read this note because I think we need to share this: 'Dave and Tim, you guys kick ass. Announce our names so we can jerk off to it.'" The fans went crazy, and my friends and I were screaming, "That's our note! That's our note!" Before Dave started "Lie in Our Graves," he told the audience, much to our dismay, "Nope, not gonna do it." We still have the tape of the concert, and it's a moment we'll never forget.

— *Mike Atieh*

DMB IN AMSTERDAM

I happened to be studying Spanish in Spain during the summer of '98 when I found out that DMB was going to be in Europe. What better place to see them but in Amsterdam? I found, via the Internet, that they were playing a few times there, and one date didn't indicate them opening for The Stones. I called the Melkweg Theater (which has a capacity of eight hundred) where they were playing and charged three phatty tickets (at $12.50 each in American money). A few trips to the travel agency and *bam!*—I was flying to Amsterdam with two friends. We sat in the front row to watch the boys play to a theater that's smaller than most American bars. Unbelievable! I was also lucky enough to find someone with a quality bootleg when I got home. Highlights of the show were the miscommunication between Boyd and Dave on "Two Step" (Boyd accidentally went on for an extra measure); Dave's strings breaking during "Two Step" and him continuing to play; the amazing jam they put together during "Lie in Our Graves"; Dave telling the people of Amsterdam how he thinks they should be meaner to us Americans to keep us out; and, finally, Dave shaking the hands of a few of us in the front row on his way off the stage after the last song.

— *Frederick Daniel Mendoza*

DAVE ALWAYS REMEMBERS a Fan

My story takes place back in June of 1996. The Dave Matthews Band were coming to Holmdel, New Jersey, to play at the PNC Bank Arts Center. Tickets went on sale the first Saturday in May. My friend Dan and I decided that we would camp out overnight for tickets. We packed the car with all of our stuff and headed out for the Arts Center. At seven o'clock in the morning we got in line with our bracelets. They called a number and I noticed that I was only about a hundred numbers away. We knew that Dave Matthews Band tickets were the hottest and would go fast. We heard rumors that the tickets had sold out in fifteen minutes, but we didn't hear any official announcement: there was still hope. Well, I was the next person in line to purchase tickets, but when the person in front of me had made his purchase an announcement came that the Dave Matthews Band tickets had just sold out. I asked if they had any single tickets available, but that was to no avail. I found Dan and we got in the car and drove home very unhappy. When I got home, I sat down to read the *Ashbury Park Press*. I noticed an entry form for tickets to the Dave Matthews Band show. I figured I would fill the form out and mail it. About one week prior to the show, I received a piece of certified mail from the *Ashbury Park Press.* I opened the envelope and read the letter; it said I had won two front-row tickets to the Dave Matthews Band concert. Well, I was very delighted, to say the least. I called Dan on the phone to tell him that I had won tickets for the show, and he had some good news of his own to share with me. He told me that he had received six tickets for the lawn from someone he worked with. I told him that I had front row. When he heard that he almost died.

We got to the show, went down to the front row, and were given backstage passes by one of the tour directors. The show was awesome. Stefan took a T-shirt from our high school that we had thrown onstage. It was a CBA Real Man's Club shirt. Dave came over and shook our hands and the show was over. We went backstage and had the time of our lives. Hanging out with the band was unbelievable. When the night was over we headed home. The next afternoon I went into my town — Lincroft — for some food. I went to the Chinese place for a bite, and I realized that Dave Matthews was there in front of me. Not knowing what to say, I blurted out, "Hey, Dave! Do you remember me?" He turns, looks, and says, "Yeah. You were hanging out with us last night after the show." He asked if I enjoyed the show and had a good time. I told him that it was the best time that I had ever had and that the show was awesome. I knew that when I told my friends that I saw Dave in the Chinese place no one would believe me, so I asked Dave if he could do me a favor and sign something for me. He grabbed a menu and inscribed "Dave Matthews." Then he took his food and departed for the next stop on the tour.

— *Brendan Connolly*

IN THE SPOTLIGHT

There has never been a DMB tour that I have missed. Since I started listening to the band about six years ago, I've always managed to score tickets. For this reason I was not worried when Ticketmaster sold out of tickets for the Madison Square Gardens shows and I was not fortunate enough to get any of them. I kept waiting and waiting for tickets to come to me, but they never did. On December 10, 1998, the night of the first MSG show, I sat alone in my room, bewildered at how I had not been able to get tickets. "How could this happen?" "What am I going to do?" The thought of sitting in my room the next night while thousands observed the band live in their full glory left me with a lump in my throat. I went for a run, trying to free myself from this horrible feeling of dread. As I was ending my run, coming up my long pebbled driveway, I noticed my friend's car in the driveway. She was sitting on my porch with this smile on her face. She sat me down and informed me that she had just been listening to the radio and had heard that there were extra seats available for both shows. I excitedly got up to make a dash for the phone, but she told me that she had already ordered tickets. I couldn't believe it. I started to laugh at the fact that I had been worried about not getting tickets — they always show up in the eleventh hour. I did my work, threw a DMB bootleg into my stereo, and went to sleep that night knowing that I would be in the nosebleed seats, but I would be hearing the music live.

The next night we caught the New York train and headed to MSG. We met up with a close friend I've seen nearly every show with who was just as excited as I was. When we arrived at MSG my friend and I headed in so we could catch Béla Fleck, the god of banjo, leaving our other friends outside; they were meeting up with some other kids. We entered the arena and were shocked by how close we seemed to be to the stage. We thought we had made a mistake, so we asked an usher to help us. What happened next was like a dream. He escorted us to the front row center, behind the stage. We were in shock as the Flecktones jammed out. We couldn't believe that we were only around six feet away from Béla. We were dancing away and screaming for Victor Wooten when all of a sudden this guy who was standing on the stage less than a foot away from us turned around and said, "They really are amazing" in that South African tang that we all know so well. My friend and I couldn't believe it: standing in front of us was Dave Matthews himself! He shook our hands as we went crazy. He laughed and then told us, "I gotta go sing. I gotta go sing—I'll be back." We were in shock as he did his duet with Béla. I looked down and saw a tall, lithe guy standing directly under me. He was just jamming away in a world of his own, and I realized he was the one and only Stefan. I screamed to him, and he got all shy and ran away. I couldn't believe this was all happening. Dave finished his solo and walked off the stage. He passed by us and shook our hands and accepted the gifts that we gave him with a "Thank ya'll. You're too kind." The set ended and my friend and I sat there bewildered. We waited anxiously for the rest of the band to take the stage and walk right by us. They did, all stopping to shake our hands and say hi.

The show was amazing, and being practically on stage was a joy. I was thinking to myself how twenty-four hours ago I didn't think I was going to the show at all, and now I was meeting the band. I kept screaming for Stefan the whole night, just wanting at least a glance. His wife and Carter's daughter stood below us, looking at my friend and me as if we had lost our minds. Béla stood next to us for most of the show, just enjoying the music with us and sporadically taking the stage to perform. The show ended and the band walked by us, thanking us and telling us what great fans we were. They came back on for the encore, and I was still trying to snag Stefan's attention—to no avail. He timidly took the stage without a glance. When the encore was done the band walked by us again; Dave took my friend's hand, gave her his pick, kissed her hand, and said, "You deserve this. Thanks." As she cried, I waited for Stefan to blow me off yet again. But, laughing, he walked by, just looked at me, smiled, and said, "You're crazy. Thank you."

The lights in MSG came on as my friend and I sat there in shock. Exhausted, we filed out and headed for Grand Central Station. Every so often we would pass a friend who would stop us and say, "Oh my God! I saw you! The spotlights were on you guys the whole time." Or, "I can't believe you guys were practically onstage! We could see you, because you were in the spotlights." It wasn't that we got backstage or that we had partied with the guys: what made the night so special was that we were so closely a part of what the Dave Matthews Band does, what we all love so much. We got to observe them playing their hearts out; we saw the communication they have with each other onstage, their jokes, their laughs. We got to show them firsthand our appreciation of their music, and we were lucky enough to have them show us their gratitude in return. Madison Square Garden will always have a warm spot in my heart, for that's where my first—and hopefully not my last—encounter with the Dave Matthews Band took place.

—*Laura Hendry*

FANS POSE AS SECURITY GUARDS

I have been to a lot of Dave Matthews Band concerts over the past several years, but the one at Hershey Park Stadium in Pennsylvania in August 1999 was eventful. My friend and I got to the stadium early to hang out and maybe catch a glimpse of the band doing a sound check. Well, as we were walking towards the backstage gate, we saw there was tons of security. There was also a Greyhound bus letting people out. I watched the people from the bus form a line and start walking into the backstage area. Nonchalantly, my friend and I got in line with these people (actually I had to drag her— she didn't think it was a good idea) as if we had just gotten off the bus, too. At this point I felt the eyes of the world staring at us, but that just made me feel even more confident—like we belonged there. I didn't know these people in the line, nor did I know what the line was for. I just knew it was a line that would get us in, not only to the show but also backstage. I told my friend to shut up and just keep smiling. We entered the backstage area, and the line of people walked towards a trailer. I realized at this point that they were going to get their security uniforms: we were with the extra security staff. I loved it—not only was I trying to evade the security people but I was also incognito among them. The line formed into a group around the trailer to get briefed about security. We seized the opportunity to walk away, towards the stage. We saw Dave and the gang do a sound check. We were underneath the side of the stage, and at one point we helped the crew move equipment onto the stage. I kept moving because I would see the head security guy, and he was not someone I wanted to piss off. So we watched and waited until the show started.

The Dave Matthews Band is my favorite band. They are excellent musicians. As the night progressed we watched from the side, and at one point we had the guts to get up onstage right behind the soundboard for about ten minutes. I could not believe the view we had of the whole stadium! The band has an energy that cannot be explained until you are onstage with them. I'm not the type to run out and try to get to Dave; I just wanted to listen to some good music. I called my brother on a cell phone and let him hear about twenty minutes of the Dave Matthews band live. At the end of the show Dave and Boyd (who I had met three summers before) walked right by me. I was very content with how things turned out that summer day. And to top it all off we didn't have any tickets for the show. We couldn't get any, even after waiting in line and trying Ticketmaster.

PS: I wrote a letter to Monterey Peninsula Artist (the booking agent for DMB) because I wanted to book the band for my wedding, in Toronto, Canada, on July 4, 1999, as a huge surprise for my wife. I got a message on my answering machine from Lynn Sengari of Monterey Peninsula that the band was unavailable for the date but thanking me for my interest. I was pretty floored that they even called back! It was wishful thinking, but I was amazed at their professionalism. Keep it real, DMB!

—Beno Thomas

FREE TICKETS
from Dave On March 7, 1999, Dave and Tim were in Santa

Barbara, California, on their acoustic tour. I'd tried months earlier to score tickets, only to be disappointed. All the shows sold out everywhere in the state in ten minutes or less. Being a huge fan, I begrudged everybody who got tickets and silently cursed the Arlington (the small venue where the concert was to be held) for seating only two thousand people. The day of the concert my friend Danielle and I went to the Arlington in the early afternoon hoping to get a glimpse of either Dave or Tim. Just as we rounded the corner to the backstage area, Dave's tour bus pulled into the parking lot! We were happy enough just to be in the same area as Dave. We caught his eye a few times, and he smiled genuine smiles that melted our hearts. A few minutes later Dave started walking over to us! We stared at him, wide-eyed in disbelief. Dave Matthews was walking over to us; he was coming to us! When he reached us he smiled and said, "Shop at the Gap today?" (We had just finished shopping and had Gap bags with us.) He then shook our hands as we introduced ourselves. I then proceeded to tell him how much I wished that I was attending the concert and how much I loved the band and his music. He smiled shyly and asked why I wasn't attending the show that night. I explained how difficult it was to get tickets. He apologized for that and then took my name down, marking that I just needed two tickets. At that very moment more people came up to us and some even jumped on Dave. He got out of there very quickly, and we were left to wonder what had happened. He came back later and had just enough time to tell us that we had tickets for that evening. We were going to be guests of Dave! The seats were great and the show was wonderful! Over three hours of storytelling and music. I just wish I could have thanked him better than I did. I hope he knows about the euphoric feeling he created in me that day. Just meeting him was amazing. I was walking on a cloud. My thank-you was too hurried because he wanted to get away from the people who were jumping on him. I don't blame him. He is a kind soul. His very presence is calming. Dave is a gem!

—*Janel Chan*

ANOTHER GREAT Birthday
Courtesy of DMB
The Dave Matthews Band summer tour of 1999 was definitely the best concert experience I've ever had. I found out that there would be a concert at the local venue on July 31st. This being my friend's birthday, I ordered tickets from the fan club as her birthday present. We scored fifth-row-center seats and decided to take advantage of our luck. We made three signs, two with messages on both sides. I even rented a limo to take us to the concert. We got to our amazing

seats, and, as the lights dimmed and the band stepped out, we proudly waved our signs. They opened with "What Would You Say," and, as the song wound down, we held up our signs once again. My friend's proclaimed, "Today is my fifteenth birthday! Please sing to me!" We watched in awe as Dave himself gestured towards us, pointing and saying something we couldn't understand. He made a quick announcement, but we could only make out her name (she had it written on the back of the sign). We jumped and screamed, not even knowing what he had said. It wasn't until later, when we got tapes of the show, that we realized he had dedicated "Help Myself" to her! He even told everyone that "none of y'all can listen" because he was "singing to Ellie." It was the best birthday present I have ever given anyone—and ever will.

—*Rachel Stratton*

SPECIAL REQUEST

This past summer, six of my friends and I decided to follow the Dave Matthews Band for a couple of shows. We picked out the show at Nissan Pavillion in Virginia and decided to follow them up north to the Hershey Park show in Pennsylvania a few days later. While we were at our hotel in Virginia, we overheard an employee say that some band was about to arrive, so we all knew right away it would be DMB. However, when the tour buses pulled in—we were waiting with our video camera in hand—we found out that it was the opening band for the show: Boy Wonder. After talking to them for awhile, we left for the show, and we had a great time. All we kept talking about on the way to Hershey was how awesome it would be if the band stayed at the same hotel as us. We didn't have concert tickets or a hotel to stay in, so we were pretty much winging it. Two of my friends who'd made the trip to Virginia decided to call it quits and didn't follow us to Hershey. (A decision they soon would regret.)

We arrived in Hershey the night before the show and picked a hotel almost twenty minutes from the park. We woke up early to try to buy tickets, and when we got back to the hotel at about noon, I noticed a large tour bus parked outside the hotel. A few hotel employees were standing outside it. We asked them who was on the bus, but they said they weren't allowed to tell us. We all just looked at each other, and without a word spoken we took off for our room to get our video camera and DMB memorabilia. When we got back down to the bus a kind bellboy informed us that it was indeed a band, but he didn't know who it was. We all sure did. We stood by the bus, waiting and taking pictures and videos next to it. We even went as far as getting our boom box downstairs with some live DMB CDs, and then we just played the waiting game. We decided we would be best off if two of us waited in the lobby and the other two stayed out by the bus. My friend Mike and I took lobby duty, and as soon as we got there we saw Boyd standing at the counter. As he walked away we snapped a few shots, and we got him on video. We even got him to look our way, and when he did, he gave us a wave and said, "What's up, fellas?" Mike and I sprinted out to the bus to let the other two know they'd just missed Boyd. After that, all four of us remained in the lobby in the hope that the rest of the band would follow. About an hour later we noticed that the elevator had been stopped on the fourteenth floor for about five minutes. When it came back down the doors opened and Dave walked out. We approached him with our tickets from the Virginia show, and he was pleased to see that we'd followed him. He signed our tickets and took a picture with us.

Now, this was going to be my sixth DMB concert, and I had not yet heard my favorite song, "Say Goodbye," performed live. Before Dave got a chance to leave, I told him it was my favorite song, and it was basically a theme for me and a past friend of mine. He replied with a smile and said, "We'll see." Well, about six songs into the show, I heard the ever-so-famous intro from Carter, and for a moment I thought I was in heaven. I kept saying to myself, "No. It couldn't be 'Say Goodbye.'" I'll never know if Dave played it that night because I asked or if it was pure chance, but I like to think that at some point when he was making the set list he remembered the kid at the hotel asking him to play it. Up to that night I was merely a DMB fan, but afterwards I was a DMB admirer. Like I said, maybe it was chance, maybe it wasn't, but it's something I will never forget. Thanks for the memories, DMB.

—*Paul Maggi*

NOT EVEN A HEAD INJURY Gets in This Fan's Way

It all started with front-row seats to the Charleston, South Carolina, DMB show on May 7, 1999. Before the show my friend and I met this very nice man—attractive, as well. Anyway, he came and found

us during the show and invited us to come see the show the next day in Knoxville, Tennessee. We both were in awe. Of course we would go see DMB in Knoxville. We were so excited that we were pumped with adrenaline, so we decided to follow the buses to Knoxville that night. I fell asleep, and the next thing I remember was hearing my friend screaming, "My car! My car! Oh shit, Tiffany—my car!" As I was trying to pull

Janessa, Dave, and Tiffany, 1999

myself up I noticed that my head was pounding. I put my hands up to hold my head, and blood was pouring from my face! I tried, but I couldn't get out of the car. My friend came around and unjammed the door and helped me out. I was in shock. After ten to twelve hours in the hospital, I left with a broken nose, a fractured eye-socket, a severe concussion, a damaged liver (from the seatbelt), and one hell of a black eye. But we were less than a hundred miles away from Knoxville, so we decided to continue our journey—head injury and all! When we finally made it to Knoxville and got our room and went to the arena, the concert was over and they were tearing down the stage. My heart stopped! I just sat down and began to cry. My knight in shining armor (who has to remain nameless) came to us and fed us, and as we were eating, Mr. Matthews came out on the floor. He came over to us, looked at me, held my face with both of his hands, and said, "But you broke it so beautifully." My heart was fluttering, and at this point I was an angel in heaven! Before he left he autographed my ticket, writing "I'm so happy you made it—Dave." He took my chin in one hand and gently kissed me and said, "See ya in Charlotte." My knees went weak. I will never be the same. That whole experience made me realize how wonderful life really can be.

— Tiffany Taylor

THE JOYS OF
LAX SECURITY

Ever since I started listening to the Dave Matthews Band, my dream was to meet the band members. My dream became a reality on May 30, 1998, at Alpine Valley in East Troy, Wisconsin. After an amazing show, I asked every security guard to help me get backstage. However, no one was willing to give up their job for a DMB fan, so I decided to take matters into my own hands. I stood around the gate leading to the backstage area: I had decided to slip through the gate while security wasn't watching. My heart pounded as I walked to the meet-

Kara and Carter, 1999

and-greet area. I scanned the crowd for the band members, and then I saw Dave Matthews in the center of a group of people. I slipped my way to the center and tapped Dave on the shoulder. He spun around and smiled. I fumbled for words and finally said, "Awesome concert Dave.

Could you sign something for me?" He obliged and signed my ticket and my DMB sticker and agreed to take a picture with me. Then he asked me if we could take another in case that picture didn't turn out. Of course I said yes. After the pictures were taken I decided to leave him alone. I was so excited that I forgot to find the rest of the band and ran back to tell my friends. On the way home I was so upset that I didn't stay to meet Boyd, Carter, Leroi, and Stefan.

Fast-forward to the following year at Alpine Valley. I decided that on June 27, 1999 I would meet the rest of the band. So, after another beautiful DMB concert, a friend and I waited around for the amphitheater to clear out. We then slipped through the same gate as I did the year before. We walked to the meet-and-greet area to find it was empty except for a few teenagers sitting at a table accompanied by a man. We asked the group if the band had already left. The man, who was DMB's golf professional, said that the band had left for their hotel in another city. He then asked why we were allowed backstage. We lied and told him we had distant connections with the band. He felt bad for us, so he invited us to DMB's hotel to meet the band. Unfortunately, the hotel was located about twenty-five miles from Alpine Valley. After being pulled over by the police for speeding, getting rear-ended by another car, and driving through a downpour, we made it to the hotel two hours later.

It was about two o'clock in the morning when we finally walked into the hotel. We bumped into Carter Beauford there. He was just about to go to his room to sleep, but he was kind enough to stay, talk, and take pictures. We then saw Dave and Leroi in the hotel bar having a few drinks with friends (Stefan and Boyd were already in their rooms). We tried to get into the bar, but our age prevented us from entering, so we decided to wait for them to come out. After a couple of minutes Leroi came out of the bar. Despite being tired and a little shy, he signed my ticket, and I told him he had given a great show. He then went back into the bar. Still hoping to talk to Dave, we decided to wait some more. Finally, Dave and friends walked out of the bar on their way to their rooms. We asked Dave for his autograph, but we were too late — Mike, DMB's tour manager, was escorting Dave to his room for the night. Somewhat disappointed, we decided to head for home, but outside in the parking lot we saw DMB's tour bus. We went and begged Mike to let us sneak a peek inside, and he agreed to let us on. We saw DMB's very luxurious living space while they are on the road. After our excitement and luck we hopped into the car and drove our DMB-happy selves home.

— *Kara Paulus*

THE "FENCE PEOPLE" MEET DAVE

Anyone who's ever been to South Park Meadows in Austin, Texas, knows it's just a huge field. On July 25, 1999, I drove seven hours from Shreveport, Louisiana, to see my first DMB show there. I'd been listening to the band for about four years, but I'd never had the money to go see them. My time had finally come! The event staff obviously had no idea how many people were going to show up, because all the parking spaces ran out. They had to start parking cars backstage (I mean literally behind the stage and behind a six-foot cyclone fence that separated fans from tour buses). We got extremely lucky and found this little spot behind the stage. As we began to walk around the back of the stage to the gate I saw a small group (five to ten people) standing next to the fence. Being a nosy guy, I decided to see what they were looking at. One of the ladies in the group said hi and pointed to the back of the stage. "That's Dave," she said. I had brought my binoculars, so I whipped them out, and, sure enough, it was Dave—standing next to Stefan and Boyd, about a hundred yards away. Right about then a security guard was kind enough to inform us that we had to "move it along." One large, fairly intoxicated young guy told the security guard that he wasn't moving. Soon a full-blown argument broke out. Next thing we know, we hear this weird South African accent coming from the other side of the fence: "Hey, guys." And there he stood. Dave himself. "Just had to come see the fence people." He had a Bud in one hand and a cigarette in the other. "You guys are yelling like you're having sex or something." He then signed a few autographs and asked, "Any songs you wanna hear?" He directed the question at one particular lady, who said she loved "The Dreaming Tree." Soooo— that's how we got it played. Then, too soon, Dave said, "You guys have fun. I'll see ya on the other side." And he left with Boyd. That's my Dave experience, and it was well worth the seven-hour drive.

—Russell "Kevin" Carter

DMB FanFare Tip #11:
GET A DMB RETAINER

It was November 28, 1998. I remember it like it was yesterday. I walked into the War Memorial Stadium in Greensboro, North Carolina, grinning from ear to ear. Here I was with great seats to see Dave Matthews, yet again. I looked up and just happened to see a man wearing a backstage pass. Nervously, I went up to him and showed him a

BETH PYRTLE

Jennifer and Dave, 1998

newspaper article that had been written about me and all my Dave stuff, including my retainer with "Dave Matthews Band" on it. I asked him if I could meet Dave, or could he get Dave to sign the article for me. Meanwhile, I went looking for a T-shirt. It took me forever to decide, until I saw this fleece with "Dave Matthews Band" on it. I had just bought it when my friend ran to me, saying, "Hurry, Jennifer—run! He came back!" I ran to my seat and there was the man I talked to earlier waiting to take me backstage. I grabbed my bag and went running down with him. I stood at the gate to the backstage, already crying from shock. I was so overwhelmed that they made a paramedic stand with me while they went to get Dave. They were afraid I was going to pass out, I guess. The guard asked to see my retainer to prove I was the girl in the article. Then they brought me up to meet Dave. Well, I couldn't even make it up the steps because I was crying so hard. At the very last step I fell to my knees. Dave reached for my hand, helped me up, and hugged me tightly— for what seemed like forever. We talked a little, and he signed my article, looked through my scrapbook, and drew me a picture. Finally it was time for him to go onstage, so I asked if we could take one last picture. Dave put his arm around me, and I put mine around him. The picture was taken, and I thanked him for everything. That's when he hugged me again and kissed me on the lips. It wasn't a quick little kiss, either. I think I melted then. We said 'bye, and I went back to my seat and enjoyed the show.

—Jennifer Pyrtle

DMB FanFare Tip #12:

STAKE OUT
THE LOCAL MALL

I heard a rumor that the Dave Matthews Band had been spotted the summer before in City Center —the mall in Columbus, Ohio— before their concert. I decided that I was going to take no chances. So, on June 19, 1999, I forced my friends to get up and get ready to go to the concert at eleven in the morning (the concert

began at seven that night). We parked in the parking garage and began our search of the mall. We had been there for about two hours, walking and keeping our

Boyd, Elizabeth (next to Boyd), and Friends, 1999

JIMMY PECK

eyes open for any "suspicious" DMB members, when we decided to split up. The group I was in got very bored and decided to go to the Kaybee toy store. As we were exiting the store, I heard my name being yelled from above. When I looked up I saw two of my friends yelling at me and pointing down to the escalator. I looked, zoned in, and there was Boyd Tinsley riding down the escalator! My heart jumped to my throat. My friends and I took off. We followed him into a bookstore and stood behind him. I couldn't get up the nerve to ask him for his autograph. He bought a newspaper and was about to exit when I got up the nerve to say, "Hey, can I have your autograph?" He was very cool about it, and he signed stuff for me and all my friends. He even posed for a picture with us! The concert that night was amazing. Dave was full of energy. It was one of the best shows I have ever seen. So now I have my picture and my autograph in a frame, sitting beside my bed. It was one of the best days of my life, and I will always remember it.

—*Elizabeth Snook*

AN ENCHANTED EVENING IN C'VILLE

It was so incredible meeting Dave Matthews! It was Friday night, January 14, 2000, in Charlottesville, Virginia. We went to Miller's, and Dave was there. At first we all seemed too freaked out to do anything but stare, including me, but I said to myself, "Here I am in Miller's, in C'ville, and Dave Matthews is here. I see him. How often will this happen again? Possibly never. Get out of your chair and go meet the guy." So I made my friend Nancy go upstairs with me to the restaurant area, and I asked his guitar tech, Richmond, if it would be okay to meet Dave, and he said, "Absolutely!" Then Dave came over from his table and he kind of bowed down, took my hand, and kissed it. It was so cute. He was so incredibly sweet and such a gentleman. He put his arm around my waist while we were upstairs in the restaurant area, then walked me downstairs after talking for awhile, and he never moved his arm away. Later he kissed me on the cheek and gave me a bear hug and said goodbye, but before that, Nancy got a picture of me and Dave, and I got a picture of Dave with Bagby and another of him with his sister, Jane.

For one picture, Dave was staring right at me and I couldn't get the film advanced, so he asked if I needed help with the camera. It was funny. He was actually posing, waving at me, and I couldn't get the darn thing to wind. The whole time I kept reminding myself to breathe. Dave was so humble and so approachable. While we were upstairs, we spent what seemed like twenty minutes or more together talking—it's hard to tell, I was in such a trance. It seemed like two hours in slow motion. He wanted to know where I was from, what I did, why I had come so far (from California), how I liked C'ville, whether it was my first time there. Then he said that he was really excited about the band's new album, and that he was looking forward to getting back on tour before too long, and that everything seemed to be going smoothly in the studio. I can't remember all of what he said, seeing as I was completely blown away and in somewhat of a catatonic state, but I can tell you he always looked me in the eyes (Oh, baby! I couldn't take my eyes off him!), and he was really attentive. I must have told him twenty times that this was such an honor, and his music brought so much joy to my soul, and I admired him so much; and I asked how his finger was. ("Fine, thank you.") I also asked him when he was coming to visit me. I told him that me and my friends have parties in DMB's honor whenever possible, and he commented, "Any excuse for a party!" He said it was always an honor for him to meet his fans, since we're the ones who listen and keep them in business and are so joyful about it. We inspire him, as he inspires us. He says he loves his fans, but he doesn't have a lot of time to visit the Warehouse — he wishes them well. That's not verbatim, but forgive me, I was freaking out. He was so gracious. Too amazing. It blew me away.

The night before all this happened, Thursday night, we got to meet John D'earth, his wife, Dawn Thompson (another amazing singer), and his band; and we got pictures with them, as well. John even took my e-mail address and promised to write. We spent probably ten or fifteen minutes talking with John and came away thinking this was one extremely nice guy. John's the guy who brought all the original Dave Matthews Band members together at Miller's by introducing them to each other, back when Dave worked there. Dave said he still has very fond memories of Miller's. This weekend was a complete thrill — quite a highlight in my life.

—Sharon O'Brien

WAREHOUSE
REUNION
Music has always brought people together, and it did just that in September of 1999. Picture a group of fifty or more hard-core Dave fans sharing Dave experiences and living life to its fullest before, during, and after the PBS *Listener Supported* show in New Jersey. Now add to this equation the fact that these fans had met each other online through the Warehouse, Dave's official fan club. Never have I met more amazing people or bonded more closely with strangers from all across the country — all in less than forty-eight hours. Dave fans are truly amazing. They are an eclectic group of people of all ages, backgrounds, and interests. For most, the only thing they have in common is their love for DMB. Plans were made weeks and months in advance to meet at a particular hotel the night before the concert; strangers with chat-room names now had faces and personalities. Funny, but there were very few surprises once we were all together. I think each one of us went into it expecting the worst. We all had been warned about meeting people online: "What if they're a bunch of freaks?" "What if they don't show up to pick me up at the airport?" Initial

hellos were followed by a late night-road trip to Princeton to meet more Warehousers. Then it was back to the hotel to meet the late arrivals, including my roommate for the event, from Florida, whom I'd never met before. Finally the day of the concert arrived. It was hard to decide what was more exciting: the thought of seeing Dave in a few short hours or meeting all of these amazing people. In the end it was a combination of the two that made this weekend so memorable. Weekend highlights: jumping from hotel room to hotel room meeting chat-room friends; learning about each other's previous Dave run-ins; group sing-alongs; wading in a pool (provided by fellow Warehouse members) in the venue parking lot; watching security confiscate our beverages from the back of a U-Haul; and finally making it into the arena for the much-anticipated DMB show.

The concert was amazing. Cameras were everywhere. Familiar faces were scattered about. A Canadian flag was waving—those of us who were there have a new appreciation for "Canuck" fans! Prior to the show we chatted about our favorite songs—the standards, the rare ones—and some wagered on what the set list would be. I believe everyone in that arena was entirely pleased when all was said and done. Plans had been made prior to the show to meet back at the hotel after the concert: bathtubs full of refreshments, people roaming the halls, Dave songs filling the air, security entirely un-pleased! Newfound friends (strangers only twelve hours earlier) hopped from room to room, laughed, and shared stories about the show and the day's events. Some ventured out for late-night skinny-dipping while others hugged, kissed, and partied the night away. My highlight, along with many other people's, was retiring to room 310, along with twenty or more others (including two amazing guitar players who could play just about every DMB song requested), where we sat and sang Dave songs well into the morning. The weekend closed with several of us heading to New York for the day; others slept in, recovering from the night before; still others got an early start to make it to the airport on time.

Each one of us has different stories to tell, favorite weekend highlights, amazing memories, and new friends who we'll always remember. Reunions will occur—relationships have grown from that weekend, some on a deeper level than others. I think it's safe to say that we all lived in a PBS afterglow for the next few weeks, religiously checking the Warehouse chat room to hear about hook-ups and other things we had missed; some of us just needed to relive the experience to make it through another day at work or school. We couldn't get our pictures developed fast enough—and then scanned fast enough to share with one another! Looking back, it's still hard for me to believe what an amazing time we had. I know I'll never forget the friends I made that weekend, or how amazing the show was, or how ridiculous most everyone thought I was for venturing to New Jersey on my own to spend a weekend with friends I met through the Warehouse. Most importantly, I'll never forget what an impact the Dave Matthews Band and its followers have had on my life.

—*Christie Terkelson*

A CHAMPAGNE TOAST
WITH DAVE
My friend and I discovered DMB's hotel last summer (the summer tour of '98) while seeing two shows at the Hartford Meadows. When the Hartford, Connecticut, tour dates of the 1999 summer tour were announced, we immediately booked a room at that same hotel, having a gut instinct that the band would stay there again. Well, we arrived at the hotel bright and early on August 6th, hoping to get to see the band before everybody showed up for that evening's concert. We waited and waited and waited — no sign of any band member. We saw lots of crew and staff, but no band members. This went on for the first two days, but on the night of the second day, we discovered something that we should have found out right away. Dave Matthews was staying about ten rooms down from us, and Stefan Lessard was right next door. We decided we would just give it one more day, and if we didn't get in contact with Dave by the eighth (the last day of the tour), we would go down and knock on his door.

Well, that day came and went and we still hadn't got to talk to him. So, me and my best friend, Scott Sommer, woke up at about eleven and ordered a bottle of champagne. We knew we needed a reason to knock on Dave's door, and we thought we would ask if we could have a drink with him to celebrate the end of a long tour — and one of his best. So we went down and knocked on his door a little after one in the afternoon. He came to the door in an undershirt and blue boxers, and we explained that we were huge fans staying in the hotel and we wanted to know if we could just have a toast to the very successful tour. He answered, "You guys woke me up. You have to realize I'm on a different schedule than you guys. Come back in an hour or so." So me and my friend apologized like crazy, and he was cool and nice during the whole thing. He wasn't nasty at all. We said okay and left. About an hour and a half later, we went back and knocked on the door. He was dressed and awake, but he came to the door with a phone in his hand, and he said, "I'm on the phone. Now really isn't a good time." Then he said, "What room are you guys in? I'll try to stop by." We told him the room number and went away. At that point Scott and I were pissed, thinking there's no way he'd come down to our room. About a half hour later there was a knock on the door. Scott answered, and who was it? None other than the one and only Dave Matthews. He apologized for taking so long and pulled up a chair. We all took a glass of champagne,and I proposed the toast: "To one of the best tours a DMB fan can ask for." Dave started laughing hysterically and we all drank to it. We then sat there talking about Dave's future plans. Dave said that he was going out to Seattle to spend some time with girlfriend, Ashley, and was also planning on going to Hawaii for a week or so and then back home to write some new songs. We then asked him if he would play "#36," and he chuckled and said, "It was in the set list last night, but we took it out. I'll see what I can do about tonight." He then apologized and said he really had to be going because he had to pack since they were checking out of the hotel. He thanked us again and left. This was definitely one of the greatest things that ever happened to me.

—*Brandon Solomon*

STEFAN LESSARD: BIG TIPPER
It was a boring, slow day at the little eatery where I no longer work. I was the only one there, it was about an hour before closing, and I had my *Under the Table and Dreaming* CD blasting. I was Windexing down the counters when someone came in the door. He ordered a large decaf latte, and I knew he looked familiar. I kept trying to make the connection to who he was. I finally figured it out when, after paying the $2.25 bill, he put a five-spot in the tip cup and said, "You know, playing that damn music so loud will get you fired." It was Stefan Lessard, and I tried to say something back, but I couldn't even speak, and he was gone.

—*Kari Johnson*

FANFARE THANKS THESE DMB SITES:

http://dmband.gq.nu

http://members.aol.com/dmblyrics

http://talk.to/huffy

www.geocities.com/SunsetStrip/Birdland/3024/firedancer.html

www2.cybercities.com/t/treefrog/index2.htm

http://openwide.nasha.com

www.geocities.com/SunsetStrip/Amphitheatre/9724

www.angelfire.com/ks/lyrickat

www.geocities.com/SunsetStrip/8934

http://haikuwarriors.webjump.com

www.geocities.com/pnp41

http://DMBHalloween.tripod.com

www.angelfire.com/va/davematthewsband41

http://davematthewsband.virtualave.net

www.gekko.org/dmb/dmbgr

www.typicalsituations.com

http://home.beseen.com/internet/underthetable

www.dmbml.com

www.geocities.com/BourbonStreet/Quarter/4110

http://web.orst.edu/~meeksjr

www.geocities.com/tool_md

www.brandeis.edu/~gittlitz

http://members.home.com/beauford

www.geocities.com/SunsetStrip/Alley/6457

http://dmb.homepage.com

www.geocities.com/CollegePark/Dorm/3255

http://surf.to/dmbmp3

www.geocities.com/SunsetStrip/Lounge/5817

www.mindspring.com/~sandman422/firedancer/firedancerhome.htm

www.geocities.com/Norqus1

DANIELLE HAVASI

Dave at Deer Creek, Indiana, 1998